W9-DCY-383

Read Aug 82

Early Days in Algonquin Park

Early Days in Algonquin Park

Ottelyn Addison

McGraw-Hill Ryerson Limited
Toronto Montreal New York London Sydney
Mexico Johannesburg Panama Düsseldorf
Singapore São Paulo Kuala Lumpur New Delhi

Early Days in Algonquin Park

Copyright © McGraw-Hill Ryerson Limited, 1974.
All rights reserved. No part of this publication may be reproduced, stored in a retrieval system, or transmitted, in any form, or by any means, electronic, mechanical, photocopying, recording, or otherwise, without the prior written permission of McGraw-Hill Ryerson Limited.

Hardcover edition ISBN 0-07-077786-1

Paperback edition ISBN 0-07-077798-1

3 4 5 6 7 8 9 10 D-74 3 2 1 0 9 8 7 6

Printed and bound in Canada

Cover photos: Dr. E.M. Addison, W.D. Addison, R.R. Sallows.

Contents

W.D. Addison

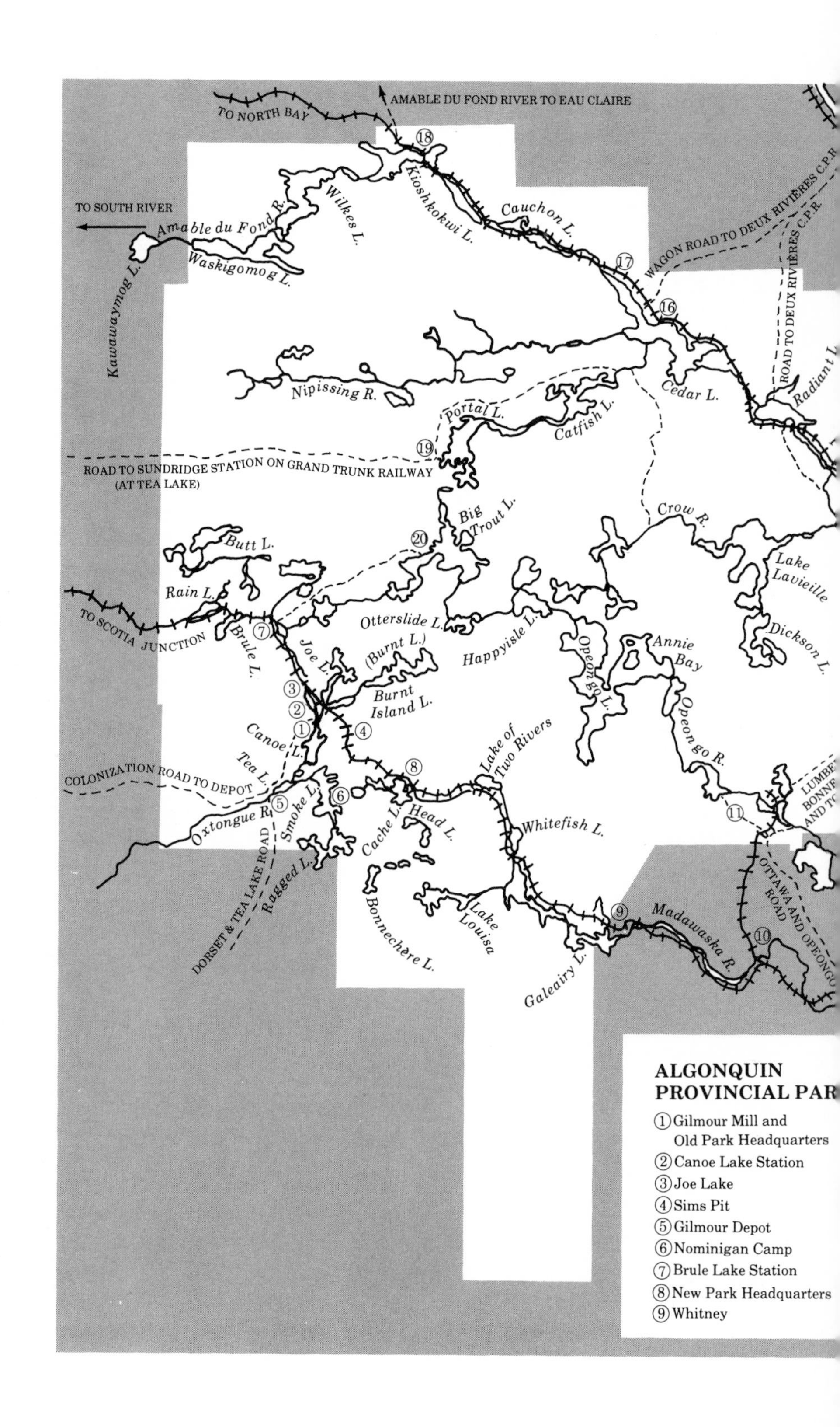
ALGONQUIN
PROVINCIAL PAR
1 Gilmour Mill and Old Park Headquarters
2 Canoe Lake Station
3 Joe Lake
4 Sims Pit
5 Gilmour Depot
6 Nominigan Camp
7 Brule Lake Station
8 New Park Headquarters
9 Whitney
TO NORTH BAY
AMABLE DU FOND RIVER TO EAU CLAIRE
TO SOUTH RIVER
Amable du Fond R.
Kawawaymog L.
Waskigomog L.
Wilkes L.
Kioshkokwi L.
Cauchon L.
WAGON ROAD TO DEUX RIVIÈRES C.P.R.
ROAD TO DEUX RIVIÈRES C.P.R.
Nipissing R.
Cedar L.
Radiant L.
Portal L.
Catfish L.
ROAD TO SUNDRIDGE STATION ON GRAND TRUNK RAILWAY
(AT TEA LAKE)
Big Trout L.
Crow R.
Butt L.
Lake Lavieille
Rain L.
TO SCOTIA JUNCTION
Brule L.
Otterslide L.
Happyisle L.
Opeongo L.
Annie Bay
Dickson L.
Joe L.
(Burnt L.)
Burnt Island L.
Canoe L.
Opeongo R.
Tea L.
Lake of Two Rivers
COLONIZATION ROAD TO DEPOT
Oxtongue R.
Smoke L.
Cache L.
Head L.
Whitefish L.
DORSET & TEA LAKE ROAD
Ragged L.
Bonnechère L.
Lake Louisa
Galeairy L.
Madawaska R.
OTTAWA AND OPEONGO ROAD

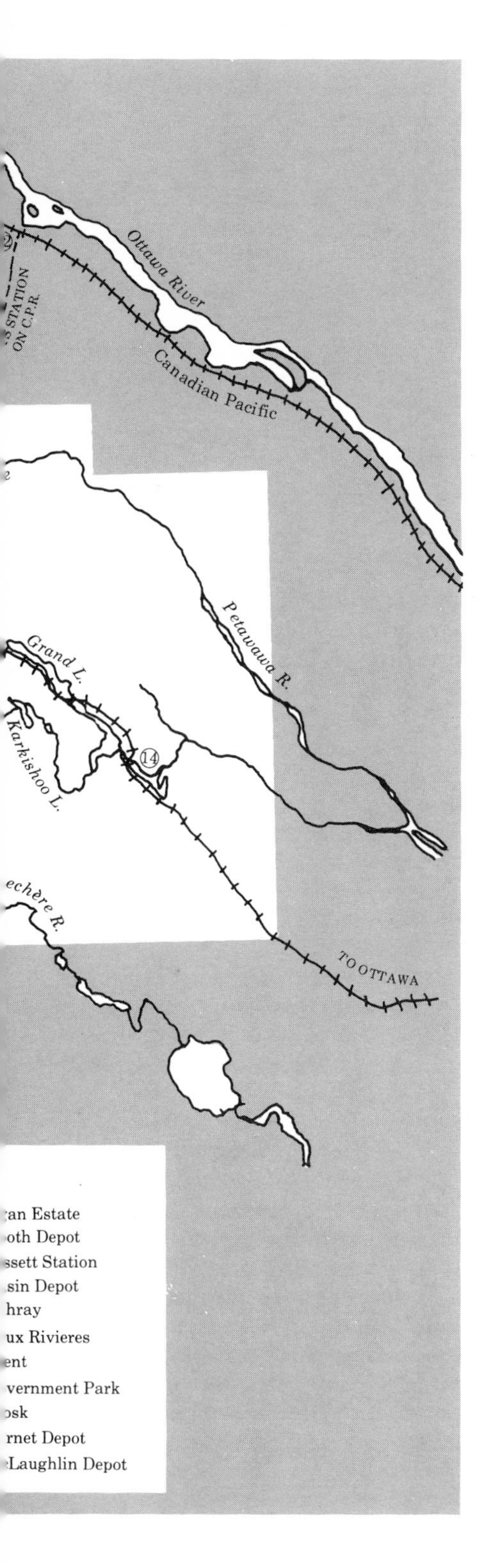
Ottawa River
STATION ON C.P.R.
Canadian Pacific
Petawawa R.
Grand L.
Karkishoo L.
14
echère R.
TO OTTAWA
an Estate
oth Depot
ssett Station
sin Depot
hray
ux Rivieres
ent
vernment Park
osk
rnet Depot
Laughlin Depot

W.D. Addison

The Time Before the Park

Algonquin Park is an ancient place, heavily worn by the gigantic forces of nature acting upon it during eons of time. Its Precambrian bedrock lies near the southern boundary of the Canadian Shield. If rocks surrounding the Park are any indication, these Precambrian rocks are about one billion years old.[1]

Recent geological history has been dominated by the glacial age when great thicknesses of ice covered much of Canada at four different times during the last million years.[2]

The last advance was about 50,000 years ago, when the Park was buried with ice up to two miles deep. The ice slowly melted, and by ten thousand years ago, the Park was finally freed of its permanent ice cover.

An examination of a topographical map shows that the land in the southern part of the Park is less elevated than the northern. During glacial times the great weight of ice on the land actually depressed it further. As the glaciers melted, the less elevated south and east sides of the Park were invaded by a branch of the Atlantic Ocean called the Champlain Sea. A great rush of water from the melting ice produced rivers larger than any known in this area today. They carried much of the glacial debris off the highlands into the lowland sea where it was deposited. In the process the debris was sorted to form the deep soils in the southernmost area of the Park—boulders, sands, gravels and, occasionally, clay.

With the weight of ice removed, the land gradually "rebounded" to its present position draining off the Champlain Sea. The hollows and valleys of the highlands were left occupied by many lakes and marshes. Today, five large river systems originate in the highlands: The *Amable du Fond* drains north, the *Muskoka* to the south-west, and the *Petawawa, Bonnechere* and *Madawaska* to the south and east. These are the remnants of the turbulent glacial spillways that fed Lake Algonquin and the Champlain Sea.

Fortunately for Algonquin Park early geological surveys had shown very little evidence of possible mineral wealth. However, around 1900 a former employee of the Gilmour Canoe Lake Mills claimed he had found gold not too far from

In the south part of the Park, pockets of deep soil predominate. This picture shows layered beds of sand in a bank of the Oxtongue River.

Mowat. "Dirty Dick," so called because he was always digging away the soil from the rocks, implied that he had been a mining engineer at one time. He gave one of the Park employees a chunk of quartz, weighing about twenty pounds. Dick maintained that it was very valuable because of the reddish colour in it and declared that his lump of quartz was studded with ruby-coloured stones that were priceless. The ranger thought it was typical of any quartz.

Several people believed Dick's claim and spent countless hours in search of the elusive gold but it was never found. Dick reportedly contacted the Ontario Department of Mines asking them to give him a fair, tentative offer, and promising in return to take them to his mine. The Department of Mines refused on the grounds that mining was not allowed within the boundaries of Algonquin Park.

The Brent Crater, which lies in Deacon and Cameron townships north of Cedar Lake, was first recognized from aerial photographs in 1951. The crater was formed about 450 million years ago by the high speed impact (possible speed is estimated at about ten miles per second) of a huge meteorite. At that time, the area was probably covered by a shallow sea.

Today, the diameter of the crater measures 9,500 feet but there is no marked crater-like depression. An observer on the ground cannot see that the feature exists, but viewed from 10,000 feet above the ground, the circle outline is very evident.

A look-out tower has been built on the crater's eastern rim and a trail has been cut from it to the crater floor, which is composed of sediments laid down when the crater was first formed. The floor is especially interesting because it consists of limestone, a rock rarely found in the Park. The only other place that limestone occurs in Algonquin Park is a small bluff at the village of Brent.

Were there Indians in the area that was later set aside for a park? One report tells us that Indians probably trapped and hunted very little owing to the lack of easy travel along all but the main water routes.[3] The heavily forested areas and the ruggedness of the terrain were great deterrents, but groups did journey into the future park territory in the early spring for fishing, harvesting birch bark for building their canoes and lodges, harvesting nuts and fruit in late summer, and during the fall for hunting big game.

The well-thought-of, proud Algonkin, or Algonquin, Indians occupied the Ottawa basin and the northern Georgian Bay regions. They were nomads and had no fixed location as did their friendly neighbours, the Hurons. When the spirit for travel or the necessity to replenish their food supply arose, they packed their belongings and started off in their bark canoes.

The fall was the time of the year that many families congregated for a season of feasting and celebrations. Immediately after, they divided into their smaller family groups and each unit set up a winter abode in a forested part of the same general locale. By this means, if food ran short, the family had a sizeable territory in which to hunt and fish to replenish their stores.

Many years later, some of the Algonquin Indian families tried to settle in a permanent place long enough during the growing season to harvest a scanty crop, but even so, they were often unable to resist the urge to keep travelling.

Probably the first European to visit the future Algonquin Park areas was Etienne Brule. He had been commissioned by Champlain in 1608 to spend a year with the Hurons in order to acquire a knowledge of the Indian language and customs. Brule's travels took him over a large territory and he could easily have spent some time with the Algonquins when they were on their fall and winter hunting grounds.

Champlain first saw some of the Algonquins on his 1609 journey. He was greatly impressed at how expertly they handled their canoes and asked his French allies who they were. Their answer was "a la gomme et kina (the gum and bark) Indians from the north." Algonquin could very well have been derived from this expression.

Four years later Champlain, with Brule and a larger party, decided to visit the Hurons in the lower Georgian Bay district. Champlain stayed for several months organizing them for an attack on their traditional enemies, the Iroquois, whose territory was south of Lake Ontario.

Champlain's 1615 attack was an ill-advised move, which eventually resulted in the Iroquois annihilating the Hurons. The Algonquins, who were also attacked, suffering a great loss of life, were forced northwards to the Sault Ste. Marie region.

About the same time, owing to Europe's excessive demands for more furs, the Iroquois territory south of the Great Lakes had become over-hunted and over-trapped and they eagerly took over the rich Algonquin Indian territory. A 1720 French map shows the previous Algonquin region as Iroquois territory, as also does a 1763 British map.[4]

Some sources say that there was a temporary trading post in the future park; this is a debatable matter, since it was preferable to have the Indians bring their season's catch out to the posts on the main water routes. By the beginning of the nineteenth century, Algonquin furs could go north to the Lake Nipissing posts, west to the Muskoka Lakes to Penetanguishene, or east down the Madawaska and Bonnechère Rivers to the Ottawa.

Archaeological work in Algonquin Park began only in 1939 when Kenneth Kidd, now Professor of Anthropology at Trent University, excavated a habitation site at Rock Lake. He found faint pictographs of one animal and some tally marks on a steep rock nearby. After 1955, Dr. C.H.D. Clarke of the Department of Lands and Forests investigated other sites and some archaeological information was deduced from them.

One of the sites examined by Dr. Clarke, at Roseberry Lake, did not have any pottery, just points and scrapers. He concluded that the site must have been an aboriginal pigment mine which could have been occupied as early as 6000 years ago.

There were several sites on the Petawawa River. Royal Engineer William Hawkins, in his report of the 1837 survey for a possible canal route from the Ottawa River to Georgian Bay, writes, "Miles from the Ottawa on the banks of the Pittoiwais (Petawawa), there is a fine range of rock, it extends about 200 yards, and is 150 feet high; on many of these cliffs figures of various animals and other devices are skilfully engraven by the Indians."[5]

Typical of the more rugged northern areas of the Park are these massive sedimentary rocks worn smooth by the glaciers.

The Radiant Lake site was excavated in 1967 and given careful investigation by J. B. Mitchell, an amateur archaeologist from Deep River. The artifacts, ranging from early pottery, flints, trade beads and scrapers to the hardware and clay pipes that were associated with the old logging days, proved that there was a possibility that the site had been in use for at least four thousand years.

There are records of several explorer-surveyors travelling through the future Algonquin Park district: Lieutenants Catty (1818), Walpole (1826) and Briscoe (1827). Each was seeking new ways of connecting the older colonies with outposts farther west by a possible canal route.

In 1829, Alexander Sherriff, whose father was a land promoter, wanted to find out if it were practicable to bring immigrants into the upper Ottawa-Huron tract of land for the purpose of establishing farms. Sherriff's party reached Cedar Lake in late August about the same time as a party of Indians had come in to hunt and fish. One of Sherriff's men had injured his leg, and he was left at the Indian encampment until the party returned from Penetanguishene twenty-five days later. Sherriff recommended that the soil in this tract was good enough for agriculture. In this he was mistaken; however, he was more accurate when he reported, "Its considerable elevation and pure waters ensure it as being unsurpassed by any other section of the country in the important requisites of healthiness."

During the summer and fall of 1835 a preliminary survey, headed by Lieutenants Carthew and Baddeley, explored the whole area but they did not go into the future Algonquin territory. Their report disagreed with Sherriff's assertion that the soil was suitable for agriculture. Baddeley was the first person to draw up a meteorological table and, from this, we learn that the first snowfall recorded in the Algonquin region occurred on October 31, 1835.

Keen interest continued with the possibility of linking the Ottawa River with Georgian Bay by a water route. Baddeley, now a captain, was assigned the task of choosing three alternate routes. David Taylor, a civil engineer, was to take the French River-Lake Nipissing route; William Hawkins, who had accompanied Baddeley on an earlier trip, was to take the Magnetawan-Petawawa course; and David Thompson, the famous western Canada explorer, the Muskoka-Madawaska waterway.

David Thompson went to Holland Landing earlier than the other two because he wished to supervise the making of the canoes. All three travelled together to Penetanguishene, the chief base for supplies, and then continued on up the Georgian Bay coast. It is interesting to note that Hawkins before starting up the Magnetawan discarded his cedar canoe because it was too heavy for river travel and transferred his equipment and supplies to a lighter birch-bark canoe. Hawkins' report included a synoptic table that exhibited the various altitudes from Bytown to Lake Huron. He drew an excellent map of his route and recommended that it was unsuitable as a canal route to Georgian Bay.

David Thompson made four detailed maps of the waterway he followed and provided the government with the first accurate picture of the whole Muskoka lake system. One of Algonquin's well-travelled canoe routes today is part of Thompson's mapping trip—South Tea, Smoke, Ragged, Bonnechère, Head, Cache and circling back through White, One Island to Smoke Lake.

Even though subsequent surveyors refuted Sherriff's claim that the Ottawa-Huron tract was good for agriculture, it took more than fifty years before the public accepted the verdict. Extensive road building opened up the Haliburton territory and each year more land-hungry immigrants optimistically established homesteads nearer to the boundary of the future Park. In too many cases it was a meagre existence. The men trapped and logged during the winter months while the women struggled with the farm work.

There were only a few farms located within the boundary of the Park: the Dennisons moved to Lake Opeongo from Combermere in 1870. Captain Dennison preferred to do more trapping than farming. After he was killed by a bear in 1881, the sons moved away and the property was sold to the Fraser Lumber Company.

Ignace Dufond, an Indian, owned a farm on Manitou Lake. It had been patented to him by the Department of Mines in 1888. The Dufonds worked very hard and sold their produce profitably to lumber companies in the area.[6]

Steve Waters, one of the first rangers to be appointed, wrote in his ranger diary, under the date November 1, 1893: "Left after dinner with Thomson (Peter Thomson, the first Park superintendent) for Manitou Lake to see Amable Du Fond (sic) he is an Indian saw him & his Brother Eneas & his squaw they have fine Farm".

The rangers were always welcomed by the Dufonds. Waters tells us about one of his visits there that had an unfortunate end. Waters had thrown his coat over a fence before he went into the house. During the visit, a curious bull pulled it off, gave it a good shake, and broke the ranger's glasses.

Eventually there was only Suzanne Dufond left on the farm and in 1917 there is a record that Suzanne was to receive one thousand dollars for this last privately owned farm, to be paid in semi-annual payments of seventy-five dollars.

Up to 1885 suggestions had been made about setting aside a forest reservation in a territory that would not be good for agriculture. All the surveyor reports showed that a suitable section would be a tract of land in the "district of Nipissing, south of the Mattawa River and lying between the Ottawa River and Georgian Bay."

Alexander Kirkwood, Chief Clerk in the Land Sales Division, Crown Lands, made the first visionary proposition. He was backed by Robert Phipps, Clerk of Forestry, Department of Agriculture, who had travelled through the district, and James Dickson, Ontario Land Surveyor, who made the practical suggestions. A Royal Commission for Forest Preservation and National Park was finally set up in 1892 with the above three men as members, as well as Archibald Blue, a mining inspector, and Aubrey White, Assistant Commissioner of Lands and Forests.

Upon presentation of their report, the Ontario Legislature, during the 1893 session, immediately passed the Act establishing Algonquin Park as "a public park and forest reservation, fish and game preserve, health resort and pleasure ground for the benefit, advantage and enjoyment of the people of the Province."[7]

Logging in Algonquin

Lumbering has been an integral part of Algonquin Park ever since its creation. This is evident in documents leading to the establishment of the Park. In an August 1886 letter to the Commissioner of Crown Lands for Ontario, Chairman of the Algonquin Park Commission, Alexander Kirkwood states:

"The timber need not be permitted to rot down . . . but the mature trees can be cut in due season to allow the next in size a chance for growth. In these ways utility and profit will be combined: the forest will be a great producer of timber, and will add to the provincial revenue."

Later, in the 1893 *Report of the Royal Commission for Forest Reservation and National Park,* Kirkwood says: "The main source of revenue will be its timber."

Before the *Timber License Law* of 1841 was revised, influential companies were able to obtain vast areas which they kept in reserve without any intention of setting up timber operations immediately. Further revisions were made in 1892 which gave the smaller companies a chance to bid at timber auctions. A large number of timber "berths" were put up for sale immediately.[1]

Timber companies usually sent cruisers, who were often senior officials, into prospective territories during the late winter when bush travelling was at its best to calculate the estimated value of a timber limit. A company based its bid on these findings.

The timber operator had to pay the Provincial Government a license fee for each limit leased and also had to pay timber dues based on the number of board feet in the logs actually cut. Each "cutter" had a horse or team of horses that hauled or skidded the log as it was cut to a selected spot on the tote road. The logs were piled, neat and trim at one end and, since the logs were of varying lengths, the other end was irregular. After the scaler measured the logs and recorded the result on his tally sheet, he stamped each log with a registered mark (X) and with the company's own stamp (for instance, "G" for the Gilmour company). The logs were then hauled from the skid-

farm
e, 1870-

ways to the dumping grounds at the water's edge in readiness for the spring break-up.

Once the lease was accepted, the timber operator had his men make an overall plan indicating positioning of the shanties (colloquial abbreviation from *chantier,* meaning temporary dwelling); they were to be not more than three miles from a cutting area. The next step was to construct the tote or cadge roads and build the necessary timber chutes on the rivers.[2]

Hugh Trainor. Foremen had to be big and capable scrappers to control their men.

It was the responsibility of the foreman and clerk to hire the men for the winter logging season. Timbermen from previous years were hired first and, if several more were needed, a foreman might even go as far as Bytown (Ottawa) in search of workers. As the logging season approached, men from all walks of life, some from as far away as the Maritimes, would congregate in certain centres. Once the men were signed up for the winter's work, the foreman checked with the hotel proprietor to make sure their hotel bill had been paid. If not, sometimes an arrangement was made whereby the lumber company paid the bill and deducted the amount from the logger's winter earnings.

It was not an easy task to keep together one hundred men who had been celebrating rather freely. Occasionally it was necessary to subdue a too boisterous man with a couple of forceful, well-placed punches. (Foremen needed to be big, capable scrappers.) Once the men had settled down they generally made a hard-working crew. Their pay varied according to experience and type of work—a new logger might earn less than fifty cents a day and his board, and an expert at squaring off a log might earn one dollar a day. A cutter who had his own horse was paid one dollar a day. It has been reported that the pay at the Gilmour Mill was a dollar-and-a-half a day in 1897.

The main waterways — Petawawa, Madawaska, Bonnechère, Muskoka and Amable du Fond—were used by more than one company during the spring river-drives. In the very early Ottawa Valley lumbering days more than one company had tried to insist that they were the sole owners of the riparian rights. This led to delays, rip-roaring fights between opposing companies' river-drivers, and even lawsuits. To avoid conflicts J. R. Booth, a lumber company owner, drew up a unified agreement for the Madawaska River and its tributaries in 1888.[3] Each company using the same water-course paid a share towards "the building and maintaining mutual dams, sluices and timber chutes; to blast rocks and other impediments that might block the floatability of the river; logs to be sorted and rafted at designated spots." Other river improvement companies were organized and convenient distribution points were set up. At last the logs could be sorted without dissension.

It is almost impossible to know which river in Algonquin Park has had the most logs floated down it. The Madawaska had always been a very busy river, yet the Petawawa, which drains more than half the Park area, might very well head the list. It is also very difficult to decide, a century later, when the peak years of lumbering occurred. It could have been about 1888, when J. R. Booth began to make plans to construct a railroad, and for the next twenty years.

William Hawkins, who headed a survey party up the Magnetawan-Petawawa course in 1837, made an excellent map of the route. He marked a timber operation on Lake Traverse, dated 1831. This may be the earliest known record of lumbering within the future boundaries of Algonquin Park.[4] (It has been said that the lake got its name because the big square red pine logs from here were used as cross-sectioned supports, known as traverses, to keep the logs firmly in place in the cribs.) Certainly Canadian logging didn't really begin until after 1763. After the financial drain of the Seven Years' War, Britain imposed heavy duties on foreign timbers as a source of revenue and, afterwards, retained these in order to protect colonial trade. Because of this arrangement, the destination for square timber was Quebec and here it was loaded on ships sailing for Britain.

Before the logs reached the larger Ottawa River, cribs (firm, compact, standard sized blocks of timber) were made, then each crib was lashed securely to other cribs until the raft reached a set size. The rafts were large enough to house the river-drivers as well as the cook and his cooking area. Because the timber chutes were too narrow for the raft it was necessary to separate the cribs and guide each one through individually. Once all the cribs reached quiet water they were once again joined together.

The British timber merchants arrived at Quebec before the rafts. Here they negotiated with the timber company agents and agreed to accept orders and prices. The timber trade was a rugged, competitive business. The merchants had to meet their contracts in spite of delays beyond their control, and the timber operators had even greater problems to overcome.[5] A timber company owner had to be ruthless, always tenacious, and eternally optimistic to be able to face the many adversities.

The very old licenses read: "Limits should extend for approximately five miles inland from the banks of the rivers and lakes." When this rule was followed the distance was not too great to haul the logs from the cutting areas to the skidways on the cadge or tote road. Some tourists got used to seeing the cut-over areas and piles of slash; others could not foresee that the new habitat, as a result of the lumbering, might be a most interesting place in a few years.

At the present time (1974) there are "cutting reservations" along public roads, along the shore of every waterway, on each side of portages, on each side of the Park boundary, and on islands. Special reserves are designated to protect the aesthetic qualities of these areas.[6]

Dams, which were constructed to hold back the water in preparation for the spring log drives, raised the water level to such an extent that many trees along the shore were killed. A few people complained about the desolate, untidy appearance of the Algonquin shore-lines. To naturalists, it was a perfect

Debris along an Algonquin shoreline.

spot to study specialized plants that liked to grow on the semi-rotten tree trunks and to study the insects that spent their egg, larval and pupal stages in the water. To artists, especially Tom Thomson, the drowned land portrayed a type of scenic beauty that was most impressive.

When a lumber company planned to cut timber in the same limit over a prolonged period of time, they cleared some land around the main depot for a farm. The Fraser Lumber Company had expanded the former Dennison farm until they had quite a large clearing. The early rangers speak of calling there for potatoes, eggs and butter. The J. R. Booth Company had four hundred acres cleared in the 1890s at their Opeongo River depot. There were fourteen buildings, among which were a blacksmith shop; stables for horses, pigs and cows; and a building large enough to hold one hundred chickens. The Hawkesbury Company on Cedar Lake had an equally large farm, started in 1870. It was still operating in 1909, for a ranger's account tells us that G. W. Bartlett, superintendent of the Park, was pleased to get fresh milk there in that year.

There were four main tote roads entering and weaving through the area before it was set aside as a park. Each was at least twenty-five miles long. There were also branch roads leading to the shanties and cutting areas. Tom McCormick, chief fire-ranger at Brule Lake, used to take his family for a cutter ride on Sundays when the bush roads would be empty. He said he could have driven for thirty-five miles without going over the same road twice.

The first shanties were the "cambuse" type of building. Their walls were log and the scoop roof was made from half-

Tom McCormick, Chief Fire Ranger at Brule Lake, used to take his family for a ride in a cutter on Sundays when the tote roads would be empty.

A cambuse camp. Note the "scoop" roof of overlapping hollowed half-logs.

logs, hollowed out in the centre. A four-foot chimney jutted out above the roof. The floor was made with small square timbers and the double-decker bunks were placed along one end and side walls. "Deacon seats" were blocks of wood, cut from hewn logs, and placed at the end of each bunk for the men to sit on while they ate their meals.

One corner, behind the cooking area, was piled high with wood for the fire. The same space on the other side was the cook's domain. The open hearth, occupying the centre of the building, was surrounded by hewn hardwood timbers. A small place in the timbers, filled with sand, was kept hot all the time. The cook buried his pots in this "bean-hole," as it was called, to bake bread and to cook the meat and beans. The fire was kept burning day and night since it was needed for warmth. It also acted as an excellent ventilator—the heat went up and the cold, fresh air came down.

The power of the cook was second only to the clerk's authority. The common camp rule of eating in silence began in the cambuse camps. With the cooking, eating and sleeping all done in the same big room, it was necessary to get meals over quickly to give the cook enough time to clean up and make preparations for the next meal.

The timber workers toiled six days a week from seven in the morning to six in the evening. Sunday was a day of rest, as well as wash day for those who tried to keep clean. Some took time to read their bibles. Even though a logger's day was long and strenuous, he was always ready and willing to go back to the bush the following season.

At the end of the winter's woods operation toward the end of March, the men who had signed up only for the logging season and all the hired teams of horses made their way along the trails for home. The company-owned horses stayed with the maintenance crew and river-drivers to clean up the odds and ends of work while they waited for the spring break-up. This usually occurred by mid-April in Algonquin Park.

The Gilmour Company of Trenton bid for a timber limit in parts of the Townships of Peck, McLaughlin and Hunter at the 1892 government public auctions. The Gilmour brothers had accompanied the cruisers when they were estimating its value and had, reportedly, said that the limit was "blue with pine." David Gilmour did his own bidding at the auction, starting with a very high bid. An opposing company's official, recognizing Gilmour, decided the "berth" must be exceedingly valuable when the first bid was so high and kept counter-bidding accordingly. The final excessive bid by the Gilmour Company was, supposedly, one million dollars.[7]

Since the Algonquin Park temporary headquarters had been constructed on the same site as one of the Gilmour shanties, that company will be used as an example to describe some of the difficulties with which a timber operator had to contend.

The Gilmour Company had another obstacle to overcome with their new limit. It was situated on the Muskoka waterway, which flows into Georgian Bay. The company needed to transport their logs south to the Trenton mill. This meant driving the logs to the Lake of Bays, then over the height of land at Dorset to the Trent water system. After that there were still two hundred miles before the logs would arrive at the Trenton mill.

The twenty-eight mile "cadge" or "tote" road from Dorset to Tea Lake dam was started about the same time in 1893 as James Dickson, Ontario Land Surveyor, was accompanying Superintendent Peter Thomson and his party into the Park. In one of the reports they had noted that Gilmours had already constructed a timber chute at Ragged Falls and another at High Falls on the North (Oxtongue) river.

Thomson had not been aware that the Gilmour company had previously chosen the same location as the Park headquarters' site for one of their shanties. Even so, it was difficult to find a reason for Gilmour building their shanty a mere twelve feet away from the Park building. P. M. Gunter, Gilmour's superintendent, said it had been David Gilmour's expressed wish that the shanty be put where it was. Later, to give the headquarters' staff some privacy, Gilmour erected a high fence between the two buildings.

Main depot of the Gilmour Lumber Company at Tea Lake, 1893.

Steve Waters, one of the first rangers, kept a diary and it is interesting to note his comments.

"Oct 20—at Headquarters find everything musty & mouldy also large Lumber camp close to House
"Oct 21—Thomson kicking about next door neighbours talks of pulling down House & moving to some other place about Thirty six men in the camp mostly Frenchmen
"Nov 26—Lake frozen over Gunter wrathy about his men Says he will discharge the whole crew
"Dec 5—Went to Gilmour's Depot for stoves & provisions terrible confusion there teams bringing stuff & others taking it away"

The spring break-up was not too early in 1894. Steve Waters tells us: April. Crosby (the foreman) men quit cutting logs." April 20—"Gilmor's (sic) Alligator... moved Crosby's gang away." April 21—"Lake clear of ice."

Once the logs reached Lake of Bays there was quite a delay getting the log booms across the lake to Dorset and even more time lost in transferring the logs by "Jack Ladder" (conveyor belt) over the height of land. During this idle time the loggers were living in tents and, craving excitement, practically took over the village.

A Dorset alligator in the 1880s. Not only could these side-wheel tugs pull large log rafts across the lakes, but by using their powerful winches they could haul themselves overland between lakes.

Dorset tramway, the foot of the jack ladder. On the left is the power house. The men guide the logs to the conveyor belt, which carries them upward to the flume. The pumps raise the water to float the logs along the flume.

One of the ringleaders thought up a plan to create a furore. He had noticed that a nearby farmer owned a huge, strong ox. He went to the farmer and introduced himself as Peter Thomson, Superintendent of Algonquin National Park. He went on to say that the villagers had approached him, asking if he would supervise clearing an acre of land for a future village park. The farmer felt honoured to be asked to help in such a worthy cause and agreed to loan his ox.

As previously planned, the ox pulled out a few smaller stumps and then he was hitched to a huge stump, despite the owner's protest that it was too large. When the ox couldn't budge such an immense stump, a throng of men emerged from the bush, shouting and lashing at the animal. The terrified ox gave a lunge, broke the chain and galloped down the path, intercepted every few yards by more men who continued to lash him. Fortunately the animal was not harmed and the farmer, a much wiser man, declared he would never again be taken in by loggers' shenanigans.[8]

The Gilmour Company had had two years of heavy expenditures without any return on their money: the cost of building the roads, chutes and shanties on their Algonquin limits; the cost of the tramway itself; not all the logs in the lake at Dorset were put over the tramway the first spring and those that were put over did not all reach the Trenton Mills that same season; worst of all was the shattering realization that the "blue with pine" limit was over-mature and riddled with ring-rot and other defects.[9]

In an attempt to retrieve some of their losses, in December 1895, Gilmour suspended logging operations temporarily. Once the Ottawa, Arnprior and Parry Sound Railway, to be completed in late 1896, was in use, the Gilmour Company planned to build a sawmill on Canoe Lake. Application was made for a "License of Occupation" to the Commissioner of Crown Lands. This license, #279, was issued on May 15, 1896, and stated:

The Gilmour Company would have "three hundred and twenty six acres . . . for a term of ten years . . . for the purpose of erecting thereon saw and planing mills together with the necessary buildings and houses to be used in connection therewith. . . .

"(f) The licensees shall keep the said premises clean and in good sanitary condition, free from filth, rubbish or debris.

"(i) The Licensees shall properly survey and lay out in lots and streets . . . on which it is proposed to erect workmen's houses . . . all dwellings . . . shall be of good construction . . . and when made of boards they shall be painted . . . or white-washed.

"(l) The licensees shall pay one-half the salary of a Park Ranger whose duty it shall be, amongst other things, to see that no such violation occurs."[10]

Constructing a log flume.

Pointers and an alligator on Burnt Lake. The pointer draws only one and a half inches when empty. With only one tug of the oar, it will pivot completely around. It is invaluable in breaking up log jams.

Since the tramway would not be used again, the boiler from the pump-house was hauled over the tote-road probably during the winter of 1896-97. Supposedly, it took nine teams of horses to haul the huge piece of equipment over the twenty-eight mile road. Birch logs were used as rollers and it was said that they wore out almost as fast as new ones could be cut.

The construction workers were put on continuous shifts (three a day) in order to have the mill in operation by the time the spring log drive started in 1897. The winter operations produced more timber than ever before. Reportedly, Canoe Lake, which is five miles long, was a solid mass of floating logs. The Canoe Lake Mills, as this separate company was called, worked day and night to get all the logs cut into "deal" lumber (three inches thick but different lengths and widths) and have it piled before the cold weather set in.

Mowat, a lumbering village named after Ontario's premier from 1872 to 1896, Sir Oliver Mowat, had a fluctuating population. At peak periods it totalled seven hundred people. A spur railway line from Canoe Lake station to the mill was constructed. The station was a divisional point with a water-tank, pump-house and sidings. It was a busy spot, active with essential business, as well as with Canoe Lake Mill employees, who spent their off-time there. It was still a busy place in 1910 when the Huntsville Lumber Company was using some of the Gilmour buildings.

Mrs. Ratan, the section boss's wife, did her best to keep the station clean but it was a hopeless task because the men kept spitting on the floor (even though spittoons were provided). In desperation she made a sign that stated:

GENTLEMEN WILL NOT
LADIES DO NOT
OTHERS MUST NOT SPIT ON THE FLOOR!

Cutting white pine. In the first picture the wedge is being placed in position.

There was a resident doctor and a hospital at Mowat. The employees asked for a school and a grant of one hundred dollars was obtained from the Ontario Department of Education. The parents also contributed a certain sum per child per month. The teacher's annual salary was $200. The Canoe Lake Mills supplied the lumber for the combined school and church, and the employees erected the building. Mowat also had a Presbyterian missionary, as well as a priest, who came regularly to conduct services.

Any community, no matter how small, has its share of accidents, illness and death. Mowat's first burial was on May 25, 1897. James Watson, one of five hundred employed at this site, was buried on the hillside overlooking Canoe Lake. One of the other workers engraved the following inscription on a huge granite rock:

Remember Comrades (when passing by)
As you are now so once was I
As I am now so you shall be
Prepare thyself to follow me.

The wording of this inscription had always intrigued the young "Canoe-Lakers." They were constantly thinking up additional lines but it wasn't until 1927, when the boys of a nearby camp were planning a minstrel show, that a ditty was composed that included the epitaph with the following two lines added:

To follow you I's not content
Until I know which way you went.

The timber market was slow in 1898 and there was no sale for cull lumber. The report that Gilmour had wasted good lumber was not true. Because the pine had been over-mature when cut, the cull lumber was piled in the millyard and kept in case there was a future market for it. Rather than sell the top-grade lumber on the slow market, it was decided that it should be held. But more piling area was needed. The only plausible solution was to dump some of the cull lumber, along with bark slabs and sawdust, into the water until the new space was solid. This piling space, as well as the old one, was given the name "chipyard." Some of the "deal" lumber can still be seen protruding out of the mucky soil in the shallow water. The ground still feels springy under foot along that section of the Canoe Lake shore.

A scaler at work.(A cold job at 20 below zero!)

Many entertaining but true stories can be told about the old-time logging days. A scaler for the Gilmour Company, working at Canoe Lake in 1898, wrote "Treed by a Moose":

"One evening when I was busy on the top tier of logs on a skidway I was disturbed by a racket made by some animal approaching through a thicket of young second-growth trees.

Gilmour house on Potter Creek. This was the checking point for supplies entering the mills and lumber being shipped out. It is now a cottage.

From the noise I wasn't surprised when a big bull moose emerged from the cover. Spotting me he lost no time in coming closer to get a better look at me. From his appearance he had likely been in battle as his fore-quarters displayed marks and he was covered with froth and perspiration.

"After he had viewed me for a few minutes I made a charge at him and gave a shout, thinking I would put him to flight. Nothing doing. Instead of scampering off as I expected he wheeled around to face me on my perch above him on the logs, pawing the ground with his front feet. It was evident from his scarred body and display of temper that he had been worsted in battle with a younger bull moose. . . .

"I knew he could not get up the skidway to attack me and I proceeded with my scaling. However, every time I got out of sight on one side, he would immediately come around to the other side and, if possible, get his front feet up on the lower tier of logs and stare me in the face. His attitude was most disconcerting. As the evening wore on and his lordship failed to slacken his vigil it occurred to me that I would be obliged to frame up some strategy to get out of this rather awkward predicament. I tried pelting him with bark and sticks but this only increased his ire. Finally I decided to out-manoeuvre his nibs and sizing up the situation I decided to coax him over to

The chipyard at Canoe Lake Mills was a vast filled-in area of cull deal lumber, sawdust and bark, created to provide more piling ground.

the side of the skidway where the logs were piled up 'even trim' and hold him there. If I could keep him there long enough I could skin down the other side where the logs were protruding owing to uneven lengths. I kept out of sight on the side I wished to entice him over to and, sure enough, his curiosity got the better of him and he came around. I gathered up more bark and proceeded to tease him. Every few minutes I would step back out of sight, then return to pelt him with more bark. By extending the time that I disappeared little by little I found that he stayed waiting for my return. When I got this stretched out to the time I figured I could make my exit I picked up my rule and tally board and went to bid him good-bye.

"I then bolted down for safety—I think I made the first hundred yards in slightly under ten seconds but, like Lot's wife, admit I peeped over my shoulder a few times. I was not sorry to part company with the big bluffer."[11]

The slow timber market continued and forced the Canoe Lake Mills into bankruptcy late in 1900.[12] Bill Gallna, who had worked at the mill, stayed on as caretaker of the property.

The Gilmour Company had the Canoe Lake Mills' lease extended another five years to 1911 to allow more time to complete liquidation. A salvaging firm from Kingston was appointed by the receivers to sell any salvable lumber in 1907. Shannon Fraser, who came from the same locality, was hired to dismantle the machinery. He brought his family up and

At the cutting area logs were loaded on sleighs, using horse-powered block and tackle. The sleighs hauled the logs to the rivers or lakes, where they were floated to the designated locations.

The mills on Potter Creek, about 1936. These mills had no connection with the earlier Gilmour mills.

they occupied the old hospital building. Both Mr. Fraser and his wife, Annie, liked Mowat so Mr. Fraser stayed on as caretaker.

The spur railroad, reported to be thirty miles long, was sold. Colonel J. J. Gartshore, head of McClary Stoves Ltd. (now General Steel Wares) claimed that he had purchased eleven miles of steel from the receivers. According to an unpublished manuscript, "They (Gilmour) had a spur R.R. track from the Canada Atlantic main line running to the shore of Canoe Lake, not far from Gilmour Mill, where they landed these supplies and loaded these onto a small tug boat to convey them to camp."[13] This distance was a mile and a half and even with railroad branches to the mill and piling grounds, it seems likely that the eleven-mile figure might be the more accurate.

A few of the better buildings were sold as summer homes in 1905. The leased acres were not cleaned up as well as the "License of Occupation" had dictated. The old brick chimney of the mill remained standing and the whole place had an untidy, neglected appearance. During the past sixty years new growth has done its part in covering up the rubble until newcomers, looking at the site, can hardly believe that the village of Mowat actually existed.

Waney lumber (partially squared with some bark left on) logged after a bad burn, being loaded on a railway flatcar. Note the white birch stakes.

The Huntsville Lumber Company used some of the former Gilmour buildings from 1909 to 1912 while they were logging on their limit west of Canoe Lake. It has been said that Annie Fraser helped to cook for the Huntsville loggers. After the Huntsville Company moved to McCraney, farther west on the railroad, Mowat as a lumbering depot was over but Mowat as a future tourist lodge had just begun.

One of the last major pine operations in the southern section of Algonquin Park was in 1925. The J. R. Booth Company logged the salvable pine that was left standing after a gigantic fire had swept through Preston Township.

Priorities during World War I caused domestic shortages and one of them was fuel. Many a household could buy only a bushel basket of coal at one time, if it were available at all. Contracts to cut thirty-five thousand cords of wood were drawn up between several municipalities and the Department of Lands, Forests and Mines in 1918. In Algonquin Park two new railroad sidings were constructed and others repaired. Ranger Mark Robinson's diaries have entries referring to the wood-cutting camps at Source Lake, Brule Lake and Rainy Lake, and there were others as well.

It was difficult to find enough bush workers in the later years of World War I. The magistrates in some Ontario courts gave a convicted man a choice of working in the bush or a straight jail sentence. In many cases the man said he would

A wood-cutting camp. Some of the men are "Canadian convict volunteers." The man in the foreground appears to have tied sacking over his feet to keep them warm. A guard stands in the background.

Piling firewood during World War I. The boy in the middle may be a Kearney boy who skipped school.

rather work and they were known as "Canadian Convict Volunteers." Another source before World War I ended was from "foreign nationals" (Europeans from enemy countries who did not enlist in the Canadian army and were interned for the duration).

Ralph Bice, a veteran Algonquin guide, does not think there were any "foreign nationals" working at the Rainy Lake camp or at any other wood-cutting camps. He and some other boys, who were all about twelve years of age at the time, skipped school and went into Rainy Lake to work. They got jobs piling the wood onto the sleighs and later, when the load reached the siding, the boys transferred the cordwood to the railway flat cars. A few of the Kearney farmers rented teams of horses to this same camp.

The last Algonquin wood-cutting camp closed in February 1921. Only a part of the thirty-five thousand cords of wood had been cut, since regular shipments of coal had begun to arrive.

During the very early lumbering days when the Algonquin area was being logged extensively, little thought was given to the future of the forest after the pine had been taken off. Now,

A sluice with most of the stop-logs out.

in 1974, the Park woodlands are divided into five management units, each under the jurisdiction of a professional forester. One of his main concerns is making certain that trees lumbered off are replaced as quickly as possible by young trees of a commercially desirable species. The amount of timber to be cut is also controlled. The logging companies who hold timber licenses in the Park at the present time must submit cutting plans for approval to the Ministry of Natural Resources before lumbering operations can be started.

Algonquin Park has regulations designed to minimize conflict between roads and logging operations on one hand and recreational use on the other. Also, logging is not permitted in the vicinity of major canoe routes during the summer months nor in areas containing features of exceptional scientific or historical value.

From Tote Road to Highway

James Dickson, Ontario land surveyor, made frequent surveying trips through the Algonquin district before the area was set aside as a park. The railroad was completed to Gravenhurst in 1875, to Huntsville in 1885, and to North Bay in 1895. Dickson made the suggestion to Alexander Kirkwood and his committee in 1892 that there was no need to spend money on roads since there were four routes by which the Park could be conveniently reached:

(1) A wagon road, twenty-four miles long, running from the Canadian Pacific railway station, Deux Rivieres, on the Ottawa River to Cedar Lake in the north-eastern part of the Park.

(2) The Opeongo road to McDougall (now Booth) Lake in the south-eastern corner of the Park.

(3) A winter road from Emsdale, on the northern railroad, to Misty Lake in the western part of the Park.

(4) The canoe route from the Lake of Bays, up the Muskoka river into the south-western part of the Park.

Dickson took a trip with Superintendent Peter Thomson on July 26, 1893. Dickson describes the village of Baysville as a busy place with a sawmill, gristmill, large dam, timber chute and sturdy bridge. More provisions were bought there, and then the group took a steamer across Lake of Bays to Dwight. Another team of horses was hired and all the provisions, except for the canoes, were put on the wagon. The men had to walk ahead, clearing away trees that had fallen across the road. In any event, the road was too rough for comfortable riding. After a journey of five miles, Hunter's Bridge was reached.

Dickson goes on to say, "Here our labour begins in earnest and hastily turning the canoes bottom upwards—for the gradually gathering clouds portend an approaching shower—as many of the goods as they will cover are placed underneath.... Each man now hastily snatching up a pack and swinging it upon the shoulder, we hurry off along the narrow trail.... We scramble, or half roll, over a fallen tree... and bend beneath another which has been torn out by the roots.... Another half mile and... we are at the landing.... We have reached our

The town of Huntsville, about 1910.

The Hayes fishing party travelling into the Park by tote road, 1895. George B. Hayes was a prominent Buffalo industrialist and one of the earliest regular visitors to the Park.

first campground. The packs are tossed off, and we seat ourselves for a moment upon them, whilst hats are removed and pocket-handkerchiefs hastily applied to reddened brows and perspiring faces."[1]

Dickson tells how his men each made ten trips across every portage because the supplies for the new Park headquarters had to be back-packed in.

In 1888 J. R. Booth, the lumber king, received the charter to construct the Ottawa, Arnprior and Parry Sound Railway. Although certain sections of the railroad were being used in the autumn of 1896, the first full run was in 1897 from Depot Harbour, Georgian Bay, to Arnprior. The railroad passed through the south-eastern section of the Park for thirty-six miles.

The name of the railroad was changed to The Canada Atlantic in 1899. In 1903 Booth sold the railroad to the Grand Trunk Railway System, reportedly for fourteen million dollars, just before the line commenced to operate at a loss.

This line was used heavily during World War I. The first troop train passed through in May, 1915, and the first hospital train in May, 1917. Freight trains, carrying grain from the West, rolled through on some days as frequently as every twenty minutes.

Maintenance section men worked around the clock to keep the tracks in good repair. An extra crew was stationed at the Sim's (gravel) Pit, one mile east of Joe Lake Station. From 1915 to 1918 there were constant "watches" at the bridges, trestles and switches to guard against sabotage. (One train wreck at Brule Lake was caused by a timberman tampering with a switch. He was later apprehended.) The Joe Lake stretch, just after a curve, seemed to have more than its share

Building the Ottawa, Arnprior and Parry Sound Railway, 1896. Horse-drawn scrapers clear the right of way.

Driving piles on Rainy Lake (now called Rain Lake).

The Islet Lake trestle.

of wrecks. A box car's wheel base could still be seen lying in the deep water below the Joe Lake bridge thirty years later.[2]

There were several long trestles in the thirty-six miles. A person's worst nightmare was to imagine being in the middle of a trestle when a train came along. This actually happened to Rose Thomas at the Cashman Creek trestle. She says: "I was only five years old and, believe me, I can remember it as though it happened yesterday. My aunt, who was with me,

Sunday was clean-up day in camp and the day for haircuts.

placed me on two long timbers. I laid down flat and she told me not to move, then she ran and got on two other timbers farther on. Neither the fireman or engineer were looking out."[3]

Work on the Canadian Northern Railway, begun in 1912, was hurriedly completed in 1915. Some foreign nationals who were interned at the Petawawa military encampment during World War I worked on railroad construction in this section. The Canadian Northern passed through Algonquin, starting at Kiosk at the northwest boundary and following the Petawawa River eastward. The Canadian National Railway purchased this section in May 1918 and used it as part of their main transcontinental route. This northern, more direct route, connecting western Canada to the eastern seaboard, gradually replaced the older Grand Trunk line.

The Canadian National purchased the now secondary Grand Trunk line in 1923. It was next to impossible to keep this ancient road-bed in repair and the trestles on Cache Lake would soon need to be replaced. This line "limped along" for a time but finally, after deciding that it wasn't financially feasible to replace the trestles, it was decided in 1935 that the trains from Ottawa would stop at Whitney. The trains from the west came as far as Cache Lake, stayed overnight, and returned the next day. It must have been disturbing for the Highland Inn guests to have to listen to the constant shunting as the cars were moved from siding to siding. Certainly the clackedy-clack-crunch din was not conducive to peaceful slumber. The last commercial run was in 1958, and in the

The east end of Whitney in the late 1920s. The school house sits alone in a field of stumps. Whitney is the nearest town to the eastern entrance to the Park and a very busy place in the tourist season. Many Park visitors who do not wish to camp stay in Whitney.

summer of 1959 four special "camp" trips were run to transport children to private camps.

The partially disrupted train service in 1935 caused inconvenience, especially for the Park staff. Mail arrived only every other day. Motorized hand-cars or jiggers were constantly shuttling men and equipment to and from work areas. It must have affected the Algonquin Hotel tourist trade from the east, although Robinson makes mention of more than one "old-time" tourist being picked up at Whitney and "jiggered" to the Algonquin Hotel. Robinson's diary also makes reference to the hand-car going for a doctor or nurse and even taking patients to the Whitney hospital.

Possibly it is merely nostalgia but, for the early tourists, there has been nothing since the closing of the railroads to equal the excitement of going by train to Algonquin. Instead of casually packing a car with necessary equipment, the trunks had to be hauled down from the attic several days beforehand and from then on, the household was in a merry whirl. Even the sooty all-day train ride was thrilling when there were so many landmarks to watch for: the first muskegy brown water above the Severn waterway; the stately white pines and granite rock at Gravenhurst; the big Muskoka lake boats at the Huntsville wharf; and even the long wait at dismal Scotia Junction was patiently endured because, from

Algonquin Park Station in the 1920s.

there, it wouldn't be long before the train chugged in to the Park stations and on to Whitney.

Such makeshift travel was not very satisfactory. The only answer was a road that would follow approximately the same route as the abandoned railroad. G. W. Bartlett in 1916 had suggested that a road be built but, owing to the pressure of war, the recommendation had not been considered.

Once it was announced in 1933 that a road would be constructed, there were countless letters and editorials in the Canadian press against such a proposition. The Honourable William Finlayson, Minister of Lands and Forests, stated: *"The Park was established for many different purposes and not only as a sanctuary for game and fish although that is extremely important.... I agree that the road should not go beyond what is necessary to provide a reasonable access to the leasees.... The receipts from rentals, fishing licenses, telephones and taxes, apart from lumber revenue, amounted to $18,468.62 last year. The summer population, including the leasees, is around two thousand people. Therefore the people have a very large investment in the Park and should be considered."*

The Brule Lake O.F.B. jigger, 1927.

Both the Provincial and Dominion governments were greatly concerned about unemployment. If the construction of an Algonquin Park road could be started, it would create many jobs as well as providing future transportation into the Park. The road was to continue on from the already completed Huntsville-to-Dwight section, to Whitney.

The construction workers were all ages. One boy who arrived at a tent encampment just outside the Park boundary in January 1933 said that the workers were paid five dollars a

Clearing the road, 1933.

month and their board. The day's work started at 7 a.m. and ended at 5 p.m. on a six-days-a-week schedule. The workers were served excellent meals and considered themselves fortunate to be fed so well.

Toward the end of the first year's work a few of the boys who had saved their meagre monthly salaries began to plan to hitch-hike to the east coast, where they would try to get passage on a cattle boat en route to Europe. Before their arrangements had been finalized, the government sent a letter stating that labourers would now be paid twenty-five cents an hour and they would be charged sixty cents a day for board. If a labourer was chosen to be a "powder-monkey" he would be paid the princely sum of thirty-five cents an hour. The boys stayed on the job.[4]

According to Mark Robinson's diary, a few cars drove as far as Tea Lake Dam in the fall of 1934 even though no gravelling had been done. One year later, 1,200 cars had driven as far as the Park headquarters on Cache Lake. By 1936 the road was open to Whitney, and 3,809 cars had used the new highway. It wasn't until 1940 that the road was open all winter. At last the Headquarters' office received daily mail.

Sandy Haggart of Whitney delivered the mail daily to Huntsville. Even though it was said that Haggart could not read or write, he made a good delivery man. He was liked by everyone and bad weather rarely stopped the mail. Haggart had previously owned an old Whitney hotel and later the outfitting store and some cottages (built by the St. Anthony Lumber Company) at Sproule Bay, Lake Opeongo, but he sold out to Mr. J. E. Avery of Whitney in 1936.[5]

Richard Miller, a biologist, describes in *A Cool Curving World* his first trip, by car, to Opeongo in 1936:

"We drove up in a 1925 seven-passenger Studebaker sedan. . . . It was a wonderful old car; its gear ratio would put a modern pick-up truck to shame as it stolidly plowed through mud-holes in top gear. . . . The road into Algonquin Park was, at that time, little more than a trail, with many low, swampy places, sharp curves, and abrupt little hills. The frost was coming out of the ground and the crooked ruts were full of water with a thin ice crust. . . . The old car lurched violently from side to side with uncomfortable abruptness."[6]

The summer residents could add their versions of many a jolting trip, as well as the continual inconvenience of putting up with improved road work. The road needed to be straightened to lessen the number of accidents caused by deer bounding out suddenly, giving no time for the driver to see the impending danger. Also it was disconcerting to drive around a corner and discover a car parked almost in the middle of the road while the occupants watched a deer. By 1948 the highway had been paved from the West Gate to Whitney and cars could at last drive without too much difficulty.

In earlier years, there had been several outfitting stores, most of them connected with the various hotels. The Parks division of the Department of Lands and Forests, set aside as a separate unit in 1954, decided in 1955 that there would be only two concessions as outlets for supplies along Highway 60

The old Canoe Lake Portage Store (left) and the new one built in 1960. This is the most popular starting-off point for canoe camping trips.

—the new expanded Portage store and the Lake of Two Rivers store. These two, with the Opeongo store, which was kept open after all, seem to be sufficient to meet the needs of the campers.

What about the roads not open to the general public? Some groups advocate that they should not be there. Possibly they do not realize that there have always been roads in the Park—in fact the four major tote-roads must have totalled well over one hundred miles. Now that the logs are transported out by truck rather than by river-drives, the mileage has increased greatly. The first tote-roads are so overgrown that it is difficult to follow the routes and the same thing will eventually happen to the present roads.

"Access" roads for forest protection purposes have to be kept in good repair. The Hydro Transmission line was erected across Algonquin in 1947 and, for maintenance purposes, a road runs parallel to it and is used only by the Hydro.

There are some roads, from outlying points, that lead to the Park boundary in different locations—Cedar Lake, Grand Lake, Booth Lake, Kiosk and Lake Traverse to name a few.

Another project that was carried through in 1963 is technically not transportation, but since the National Research Council of Canada had to construct an extension of the road to the Radio Observatory site, it will be included here. The only part of the road that is paved is in the immediate vicinity of the Observatory. This was done to simplify snow removal and to cut down on maintenance.

The lease of this plan is for one hundred and thirty-five acres. The complex dish-shaped metal antennas, one of them ranking among the world's largest (150 feet across), had to be set up in a remote and protected area in order to remain free of man-made electrical interference. It is known as the Algonquin Radio Observatory. Since large radio telescopes are in short supply, the Observatory is in constant use by National Research Council and university scientists. They frequently carry out unique co-operative research projects with scientific groups in other parts of the world.[7]

National Research Council radio telescope at Lake Traverse.

An emergency landing strip was established by the Dominion Department of Transport at Lake of Two Rivers in 1935. It was part of a Trans-Canada scheme of emergency landing fields and was not for use commercially. Private planes with restricted permission occasionally land but it is not used extensively.

Superintendent Frank MacDougall's daily patrolling by plane, beginning in May 1931, was of great assistance in every aspect of the rangers' work. In addition to fire protection, it was used for many other purposes: for mercy flights; for government officials who had to fly to save time; and to transport research men and their equipment to their study areas.

The first hangar, erected in 1931 behind Park headquarters on Cache Lake. The noise from the planes was a nuisance to cottagers; a larger hangar was built on the less populated Smoke Lake in 1939 and is still in use. Right, Superintendent Frank MacDougall and the first Algonquin Park patrol plane.

For a time private planes were taking tourists directly to their favourite fishing lakes that had previously been accessible only by canoe. Such a fast travel route meant that there might be over-fishing in certain lakes (see section on fish). In 1956 the Department of Lands and Forests took drastic action and ruled that private planes could land only on certain lakes on the external boundary of the Park and from there the fishermen would have to travel into Algonquin by canoe.

More unforseen tasks for the planes will continue to arise. For instance: who would ever have thought, in 1931, that planes would be transporting garbage out of Algonquin in the 1970s?

Forest Rangers and Other Staff

ALGONQUIN

NATIONAL PARK

OF ONTARIO

Notice is hereby given that the following lands in the District of Nipissing, namely:—the Townships of P[illegible]ston, Dickson, Anglin, Deacon, Sproule, Bower, Freswick, Lister, Canisbay, McLaughlin, Bishop, Osler, Pentland, Peck, Hunter, Devine, Biggar, Wilkes, all that portion of Finlayson, east of the side road between lots 20 and 21 in the several concessions thereof; all that portion of McCraney, east of the side road between lots 15 and 16 in the several concessions thereof; all that portion of Butt east of the side road between lots 15 and 16 in the several concessions thereof; all that portion of Paxton east of the side road between lots 15 and 16 in the several concessions thereof; all that portion of Ballantyne east of the side road between lots 20 and 21 in the several concessions thereof, except lot 21 in the 5th concession; all that portion of Boyd south of the line between concessions 10 and 11; the west half of the Township of Fitz-Gerald comprising lots 1 to 20 in concessions 1 to 14 inclusive; the west half of the Township of White, say lots 1 to 20 in concessions 1 to 14 inclusive; the west half of the Township of Niven, say lots 16 to 38 in concessions 1 to 14 inclusive; the west half of the Township of Clancey, say lots 16 to 37 in concessions 4 to 15 inclusive, the north 80 acres of lot 36 and the north 72 acres of lot 37 in the 2nd concession, and lots 35, 36 and 37 in the 3rd concession; the eastern part of the Township of Lawrence; the Township of Nightingale except the south-east corner; and the north-west part of the Township of Airy, have been set aside as a Public Park, Forest Reservation and Fish and Game Preserve, under the name of "The Algonquin National Park of Ontario," by virtue of 56 Vic., chap. 8.

THE SAID ACT STRICTLY PROHIBITS

1. Carrying or using firearms or explosives within the Park, except as provided by Regulations.
2. Hunting or Trapping therein.
3. Fishing with net, trap, spear or night line.
4. Fishing with hook or line without license from the Minister of Lands, Forests and Mines or Superintendent of the Park.
5. Mining exploration or prospecting for minerals.

The Superintendent and Park Rangers are empowered to arrest and bring to trial or remove from the Park any person found violating the said Act or regulations, or carrying or having in his possession any fishing nets, traps, spears or night lines, furs, skins, or peltries, firearms, or explosives, and to seize and confiscate the same.

The penalty for violating the said Act or Regulations is a fine not exceeding $100.00 for each offence, or in default of payment thereof, imprisonment for a term not exceeding three months.

All persons are required to govern themselves accordingly.

The co-operation of the public is invited in preserving the timber, game and natural beauty of the Park, and in carrying out the objects for which it has been established.

F. COCHRANE,
Minister of Lands, Forests and Mines

Toronto, August 15th, 1911.

Alexander Kirkwood, Chairman of the Algonquin Park Commission, described, in his report to the Commissioner of Crown Lands in 1886, different methods for managing the future "Algonkin Forest and Park." In addition, he put the duties of the Park staff in rhyme as follows:

"You shall true liegeman be
Unto the King's Majesty:
Unto the beasts of the forest you shall no hurt do,
Nor to anything that doth belong thereunto:
The offences of others you shall not conceal,
But to the utmost of your power you shall them reveal
Unto the officers of the forest,
Or to them who may see them redrest:
All these things you shall see done,
So help you God, at his holy doom."

When the Park Act was transferred from the planning stage to reality in 1893 the name chosen was Algonquin National Park. The "National" was changed to Provincial in 1913.

Peter Thomson, a road and bridge builder, was appointed the first Chief Ranger at a salary of six hundred dollars a year. Thomson was given the title of Superintendent in the spring of 1894 with a salary of one thousand dollars. "He was to be furnished with a small log house in the Park in which to live and be supplied with firewood from the down timber but not other supplies. . . ." "You and those acting under you are authorized to protect the Park, Game, Fish, etc as per the terms of the Act of which you have a copy. You will see that the law is observed on this behalf; indeed your appointment as Chief Ranger implies this."

Peter Thomson was accompanied by James Dickson, an Ontario Land Surveyor who had previously surveyed several townships in the area, three rangers, Stephen Waters, William Geall, Tim O'Leary, and three helpers.

The party travelled up the north branch of the Muskoka River (later called "Oxtongue"), through South Tea Lake and arrived at the head of Canoe Lake in mid-afternoon on August 2, 1893. They pitched camp on a bluff on the east shore about a

Among the earliest pictures of travellers in Algonquin Park, this photograph shows James Dickson in the camp at Canoe Lake in 1893.

quarter of a mile from the inlet of the river. The next day, while the men were fitting up axes and getting ready for work, Thomson and Dickson make an examination of the whole locality and selected a site for the headquarters' house on a slight elevation on the west shore—almost directly across the lake from their campsite. This site was "adjoint to the survey of the Booth railway which skirts around the north end of the lake."[1]

The location seemed ideal because it was on the main waterway from the Muskoka District, through the Park to the Petawawa River system; the Gilmour Lumber Company, Trenton, had started building a tote road from Dorset to South Tea Lake where they planned to establish their main depot; it would not be far from the proposed railroad and the Algonquin Park staff could get mail and supplies regularly from both these sources.

Peter Thomson's first report in 1894 says: "After setting the men to clear the place, get out timber for the buildings, etc., Mr. Dickson, myself and one of the rangers (Stephen Waters) set out on a tour of inspection for the purpose of locating sites for shelter lodges."

The men who stayed at Canoe Lake were expert woodsmen and "shingle weavers" and by the end of August they had finished a "substantial, hewn log building, 21′ by 28′ with a hewn timber floor and a 'scoop' roof. Beds and tables were made, using only an axe and draw-knife. The house was to be heated by a specially constructed sheet iron stove."[2]

In September, James Wilson, Superintendent of the Queen

Victoria Niagara Falls Park, was asked to accompany Peter Thomson on another inspection trip to choose sites for more shelter lodges. It was essential to have shelter huts located about ten miles apart. Then rangers on patrol would never be too far from a shelter hut if a storm came up.

Wilson's 1894 report made a few suggestions:
"For many years several parties of tourists have been visiting the territory and spending some time each season revelling amid its health-giving charms and doubtless the new improved conditions will awaken a much wider interest and attract others. For this reason the design of the depots (shelter huts) should provide some spare room for the shelter of tourists in case of need."
In the early years tourists frequently were granted permission to use a shelter hut until one wondered if "in case of need' had become "in case you desire."

Remarks written in Steve Waters' diary give some indication of the difficulties that had to be overcome on this trip:

"Three days on trip now. Slow work cutting portages. Finally reached Opeongo and gone to Fraser Lumber Company camp for supplies—got butter, eggs, pork and potatoes. Opeongo very rough, Thomson wrathy three days wind bound... O'Leary snored like a steam calliope... carried canoe to (White) Trout Lake three miles up to our knees in water in come places....

"October 20—at Headquarters find everything musty and mouldy also a large lumber camp close to the House Thomson kicking about next door neighbours talks of pulling down House and moving to some other place about thirty six men in

Of the first shelter huts, only this one at Rain Lake was made from lumber. Others were of squared logs. Standing in the doorway are rangers Grigg (left) and Waters. In front of the cabin are George B. Hayes of Buffalo and, to the right, three Indian guides.

A visit to an old lumber or construction camp probably taken over by the Park staff, summer 1898. The man second from left wears a ranger's badge and the man on the right is G. W. Bartlett, superintendent of the Park.

the camp mostly Frenchmen. . . . I do the cooking while at Headquarters always forget to put salt in the porridge."

Another exploratory trip was started as late as October 23 back across the Park. Waters tells us that the men were kicking because they were afraid they would be frozen in. In fact, not only did the ice cut a hole in one of the canoes but more than once they had to portage around a lake to avoid ice on the smaller lakes and very rough water on the larger lakes. The party did not get back to Headquarters until the middle of November. Before James Wilson left on November 14th Waters made a list of all the lakes and portages the party had covered and the lengths of each.

Just two days later when Thomson and the rest of the party were ready to leave Headquarters there was three-quarters of an inch of ice on the lake. It took a Gilmour pointer all day to make the ten mile trip to the depot when it usually could be done in two hours.

Steve Waters was the ranger who was stationed at the Headquarters during the first winter of 1893-94. The Gilmour Company agreed to pay half the resident ranger's salary since part of his job would be checking to make sure there were no violations as stated in the timber lease.

Waters was a man of action and he found the winter long

and tedious. There had been several heavy snowfalls totalling fifty-five inches and that made it almost impossible for him to do daily patrolling. Also his "beat" was much too large for one man to check adequately.

Unknown to Waters, one of the loggers at the Hickey's Lake shanty (about five miles away) had come prepared to set out a trap-line as a side venture. The trapper-woodcutter got up much earlier than his fellow workers, hurried out to check his traps and often got any captured animals skinned and tacked on a tree to dry before going back for breakfast.

On May 14, 1894, Peter Thomson was appointed superintendent, and a new man, John Simpson, came in to be chief ranger. Waters, in his diary, refers to Simpson as "good-hearted but a queer stick."

Peter Thomson died in his mid-fifties at Canoe Lake on September 5, 1895. John Simpson, also in his late forties, was named superintendent and Tim O'Leary was made the chief ranger.

Canoe Lake was a very busy place for the next four years. Gilmour's "License of Occupation" was authorized in March 1896 and they made immediate plans to build a sawmill. Section (s) says "the licensees must remove the Headquarter buildings and replace them with good, warm frame buildings with shingle roofs, finished doors and windows according to plans and specifications furnished by the Department of Crown Lands to a location on the east side of Canoe Lake.... They are to clear the land required and make a convenient road and bridge to join the road of the licensees to the adjoining railroad station . . . the said work and material to be the expense of the licensees."

After Wilson had returned from his inspection trip he sent a

From 1907 to 1909 the subheadquarters was in a Gilmour company building. Mark Robinson relaxes on the bunk. Note his camera, revolver and other paraphernalia hanging on the wall.

report to the Commissioner of Crown Lands. In it he recommended that a new site for headquarters be selected and suggested a location across the lake. This recommendation must have been accepted because some clearing had been done. R. P. Little, in his article "Some Recollections of Tom Thomson and Canoe Lake," says: "This site had been selected for the Park Headquarters but later abandoned. The ground had been dug up and some lumber piled to one side."[3]

There is no record as to why Cache Lake was chosen for the permanent Park headquarters. The land might have been cleared for a depot during the building of the railroad. The inspectors and officials who came in to check construction progress were very impressed by the beauty of the lake with its many wooded islands. The surrounding hills had never been burned or lumbered—a vivid contrast to Canoe Lake. It was a disadvantage to have the headquarters off the main waterways but probably the scenic beauty was the deciding factor. The lumber and supplies for the new buildings arrived from the Egan Estate mills in November, 1896.

Steve Waters' diary states that Superintendent Simpson was still at Canoe Lake in the early spring of 1897 but, by late fall, he was stationed at Cache Lake and the Canoe Lake "berth" had become a sub-headquarters. From 1899 until the spring of 1909 the small squared-log building that some say was previously the Gilmour office was used by the rangers. "The Manse" (because the Presbyterian missionary always stayed there when he came in to conduct church services) was used as the sub-headquarters from 1909 to 1911.

The two years before Thomson's death had not been

In 1909 subheadquarters moved next door to the building known as "the Manse," one of the few Park buildings with plastered walls. Mark Robinson papered the walls in May 1909. Left to right, Dan Ross, Mark Robinson, Philip George.

"The Manse," the Park subheadquarters at Canoe Lake Berth, 1909 and now. New trees have grown and the lake level is considerably higher. It is now a cottage.

F. McD.

Toronto, Nov., 15th, 1907.

Dear Sir,-

I am directed by the Honourable the Minister of Lands, Forests and Mines to inform you that you have been appointed a ranger in Algonquin Park, and you are requested to report for duty to Mr. G. W. Bartlett, Superintendent of the Park, at Algonquin Park Station on the 1st December proximo. You will be subject to the orders and direction of the Superintendent of the Park and of this Department, and your appointment is made conditional upon your proving in every way competent and trustworthy. Should you prove to be unsuitable or should you at any time no longer be required, your services may be dispensed with by the Department without notice. Your pay will be at the rate of $50.00 per month and you will find your own board and clothing. Your reasonable travelling expenses from your present address to the Park headquarters will be paid by the Department, and I enclose herewith expense sheets upon which you will make a statement of same in duplicate, together with all receipts or vouchers for sums paid by you in excess of $1.00.

2

Kindly acknowledge receipt of this letter and advise your acceptance or otherwise of the above terms.

Yours very truly,

Deputy Minister of Mines.

Mark Robinson, Esq:
New Flos, Ont.

enough time to get the administration organized. By 1897 the Commissioner of Crown Lands was becoming alarmed at the unfavourable reports concerning the management of the Park. The adminstration under Superintendent Simpson was too relaxed and very little progress was being made in developing the Park.

G. W. Bartlett was appointed as superintendent and he took over his duties on August 5, 1898. John Simpson reverted back to being chief ranger and was superannuated shortly afterwards. Bartlett, at the time of his appointment, was a foreman with the J. R. Booth Lumber Company. He was a man of action with a long experience in organizing men in road, bridge and railroad construction.

Bartlett realized he needed more men on the staff before he could achieve very much. He hired some former trappers because they knew the country well and could stand up to the rigorous life. Others joined the staff because they had been advised to do outdoor work for health reasons.

Mark Robinson came from Simcoe County and joined the staff in November 1907. Mark had been seriously ill the previous spring, and the doctor had advised outdoor work in the north.

One of Robinson's first assignments was a snowshoe trek to re-check the eastern boundary survey line of the Park. He was accompanied by another new ranger, George Rodgers. When they started out the thermometer registered forty below zero—definitely a very cold day, even for January. All went well until late in the afternoon. Both men were snowshoeing up a steep incline when suddenly the snow embankment they were on began to slide down into the gulley below. George landed comfortably in deep snow but Mark had the misfortune to get stranded on a sharp broken limb of a downed tree. The impact tore a nasty gash in his abdomen. George hastily closed and bandaged the cut as best he could, built a fire, and left Mark to rest while he went ahead and packed a trail to the railroad track. On their return to headquarters Dr.

William Bell stitched the wound and congratulated George on his first aid. It wasn't until later that the men were told their trip had been a test as to whether they could cope with vigorous winter travel. A couple of the "old-time" rangers stationed at Headquarters grumbled a little and wanted to know why the two rangers had had to start out in such severe weather because, now, all rangers would be expected to do the same.

Dr. Bell first came to Algonquin Park around 1900 to convalesce from an illness. He became interested in mapping and Bartlett asked him if he would join the staff and make a detailed canoe-trip map. The Highland Inn's brochure for 1930 included this same map. Many changes have been made in renaming lakes. Some were necessary—e.g., there were two Tea Lakes. The name of one of the lakes, Manitou, expressed the beauty and mysticism of the lake and the Park lost a link with the past when it was changed to Wilkes (largest lake in the township of Wilkes). Manitou had been the name chosen by the Indian family, Dufond. When they first arrived at the lake in 1888 they had found a large water snake on their property and since a snake is a symbol of Manitou, the Great Spirit, it was appropriate.

During Bartlett's superintendency there were more than fifty rangers appointed to the staff, some for short periods and others for years.

Dan Ross had been an expert river-driver. He is mentioned in Ralph Connor's book *The Man from Glengarry*, as Big Dan. Ross retired in 1913 after being on the staff for nearly twenty years.

Bob Balfour was known as a "gentleman beyond par." Before joining the Park staff in 1895 he had worked for the McLaughlin's Lumber Company. He was an expert log cabin builder and supervised the building of many of the shelter houses.

Jim Bartlett, son of the superintendent, liked the bush life. He and Mark Robinson worked at inventing the live beaver trap that is still in use today. The live trap was a simple affair, and beyond giving the beaver the surprise of a lifetime and a few uneasy moments about the future, it did him no harm. Just visualize a large club bag opening right down to the ground with the sides made out of two-inch iron rings linked together instead of cowhide. The "club bag" is laid out flat in the water. The beaver, when passing over it, pushes on the release and the powerful springs close the trap up with a bang.

There were three Park rangers on staff whose family name was "Ranger." Albere, the father, looked after the dog team and often drove it when Mr. Bartlett went on winter patrols. Telesphore and Peter, the sons, had their father's sense of hu-

To publicize the Park, G. W. Bartlett proposed in 1908 to live-trap beaver and send them to zoos and animal collections all over the world. The cost and work involved in trapping and shipping the animals, and the fact that many died in transit, led to the abandonment of the project in 1918. Here Park staff are shown with two of the traps and, beneath the traps, the shipping cages.

mour and worked faithfully on the staff in the northern section of the Park.

Zeph Nadon was known to be one of the best bushmen in Ontario. He was a member of the Park staff for more than forty years, retiring around 1950. Bartlett posted Nadon to the northern section of the Park where it was richly populated with fur-bearing animals. He became well-known for his tenacious efforts in tracking down poachers. His motto was to do all he possibly could to assist travellers in the Park.

Arthur Briggs was a later arrival to the Park staff in 1919. He was an excellent photographer and many people thought his photographs were superior to the best commercial ones. Unfortunately most of them were destroyed in later years when he decided that they were not important enough to keep. Briggs was the only ranger to receive a medal for bravery. Normally rangers considered rescues as part of their daily work but Briggs almost lost his own life in this hazardous attempt. Three Minnesing Lodge staff women had gone across the lake for a picnic and didn't return until after dark. As the canoe neared the hotel dock, they accidently dumped the canoe. Two of the women reached shore safely but the third one panicked and went under. By the time people heard the cries for help, the woman had been under more than a minute. One or two of the guests were good swimmers and they immediately attempted to locate the body. However, the water was twenty-five feet deep and they were having difficulty reaching the bottom.

Arthur Briggs, whose shelter house was nearby, had been ill in bed all day. Even so he insisted on going over to help look for the body. Briggs was able to reach the bottom, found the body, and brought it to the surface. With the assistance of one of the guests who was a doctor the two men successfully resuscitated the girl. The rescued girl did not seem to have any after effects from the ordeal but it took Briggs several days to recover.

To illustrate the difficulties of winter-patrol and the importance of having the shelter huts situated a day's journey apart, Mark Robinson wrote "Through Algonquin Park with a Dog Team" for the January 3, 1913 issue of *Saturday Night*. In it he describes a patrolling trip he took in January and February of 1910 with Superintendent Bartlett and his son Jim.

"We were travelling on snow-shoes with a sleigh and team of dogs. The sleigh we built strong and light, shod with aluminum. When loaded with our bedding and provisions the whole weight was only 325 pounds. We had two dogs, Judy, a ten-month-old Dane, as leader, with Jack, a veteran Dane, hitched to the sleigh."

The rangers took the train to Brule Lake, where they hitched the dogs to the sleigh and started their trip.

"We . . . entered the forest taking a road used by the lumbermen. This road we were to follow for about twenty miles. Then we would have to break a trail over hills and lakes and through valleys. The road took us across MacIntosh Lakes . . . to MacIntosh Marsh. We went on to White Trout Lake, where we saw many wolf tracks. . . . Going down the Marsh we saw several otter playing on ice near open water. . . . Many times a bunch of deer would dash across the trail. These were trying times for Jimmy, as the dogs were always ready for a spurt when deer hove into view. Crossing White Trout Lake we met a teamster, who informed us that we would have a hard time once we reached Longer Lake. . . . Two of their teams with loads of provisions had gone through the ice on that Lake the very same day. They had managed to save the horses but the provisions were badly damaged.

"On reaching Longer Lake we found the slush on the ice knee deep. We had to take the dogs out of the sleigh and unload a portion of our stores and take the whole thing ashore ourselves. That night we put up at White Trout Shelter House.

"Going down Longer Lake, Superintendent Bartlett went through the ice, but managed to get out with only his feet wet. . . . We followed the trail along Alder Creek for about half an hour, when our sleigh broke down. We were obliged to leave our load and go on to Burnt Lake Lumber Depot, two miles away. . . . We discovered that Ranger Balfour had left his sleigh there, and so we were well provided for once more.

"We returned with the sleigh . . . and made repairs. Dividing up the load between both sleighs we got back to the depot where we made further repairs. . . . Then we . . . started out to cross Burnt Lake. But we were warned against it.

"We . . . found the slush deep with many air holes in the ice. It was next to impossible to keep the sled on the snow shoe track. At every step we went deep into slush and our shoes were loaded with ice. . . . After travelling about three miles Mr. Bartlett decided . . . to unload all but the necessary bedding and provisions for the night. . . . We pushed on and reached Burnt Lake Shelter House just as the sun set behind the hills.

". . . Ranger Balfour had a fine supply of dry wood. In half an hour's time we were enjoying a feed of hot tea, toast and bacon. Soon afterwards we heard the wolves on the lake. They had discovered our stores and were making merry music. . . .

"After a hearty breakfast we started out to bring in our supplies off the lake. . . . We found that the wolves had travelled all around our stores but had not come closer than about thirty feet."

The rangers returned to the Shelter House and spent a week there exploring and rebuilding the sleigh. On February 5, they started for Nipissing River Shelter House.

"Leaving Brownie Lake, we had to help the dogs by pulling on a long rope to get up the steep hills. . . . We found the travelling very bad, the snow being five feet deep and soft. We sank from twelve to sixteen inches on our snow-shoes. . . . Our dogs had to quit about half a mile from our destination. . . . We resolved to break our trails a day or so ahead, although this meant going over the trail three times.

"We spent a jolly evening at Nipissing Shelter House and on Sunday morning we walked about four miles over the trail toward Amable Dufond Shelter House. In passing a pretty nook in the evergreen shrubbery on the banks of the Nipissing, we noticed a square piece of board nailed to a tree. The

inscription, which was burnt into it, stated that beneath lay the body of a young man who had met his death in the rapids below. We looked down at the rushing water. . . . The noise of the rapids seemed to sing a fitting requiem in those beautiful and lonely surroundings.

". . . On Monday morning we all started for Amable Dufond, crossing Osler and Tillie Lakes. . . . We had to cut hundreds of small trees out of the trail, as they were loaded with snow and bent over the trail so as to block it completely. At last we reached the Shelter House and all stood looking a little ruefully at the shack."

Evidently the Shelter House was not in good repair, for when the men returned to it on Tuesday, they "spent the afternoon chinking up the holes in the walls with moss, and cutting wood." The next day, the rangers broke the trail from Tillie's Lake to Lake Erable.

"Long before daylight, wolves made the woods ring with their howls and all during forenoon they hung on our trail. Our splendid dogs would whine and look at us appealingly and then try to make a dash into the woods where the howling brutes kept out of sight. . . . We arrived at Maple Lake Shelter House toward evening. Our provisions were getting low. Next day, we broke a trail to Kioshkoqui Lake, and the following day made a dash and reached the Shelter House there at noon. Ranger John Sauvie had seen us coming across the lake and had a hot dinner for us.

"We had now crossed the Park to the extreme north side. . . . Sunday morning we made a count of Ranger Sauvie's cats, and found him the proud possessor of no less than twenty-eight. They had come to the shelter from a lumber depot close by, when it was vacated by the lumbermen."

On the return journey, near Lake Cauchon, "We passed one of the camps and all the men turned out to pass their opinion on our team. They were a fine stalwart rollicking bunch of good natured fellows. All around lay the results of their season's work, thousands of white pine logs in some places piled up twenty deep, ready for the break-up."

The rangers ran low on food almost a month after they had started the trip. "We still had a handful of rice, a cup of sugar, one drawing of tea, and a pound of dripping from the bacon, but there was lots of game in the woods and we didn't worry.

"About half an hour later, we found the new shelter house (at Hogan Lake), and we were soon inside it. We found a good supply of fire-wood, and best of all, about twenty pounds of ship-biscuits. Our faithful dogs received a fair ration at once. The next four meals consisted of ship-biscuits soaked in water and then fried in bacon fat. It tasted mighty good."

On February 25, they were making their way to White Trout Shelter House. "The going was good, and as we crossed

Lake Lamuir, we thought we heard the sound of axes. A moment later, we saw a team and a number of lumberjacks, and in about ten minutes we were on a first class ice road. We tied our shoes on the sleigh, and the Superintendent had Jimmy jump on and go to the camp to get provisions to take us out."

The rangers pushed on to White Trout Shelter House. "Soon after our arrival a storm started and turned to rain during the night. Sunday morning found it still raining. . . . On Monday morning, the 28th of February, we set out for headquarters. We had a road to Brule Lake, but found it six inches deep with water. Off the road it was much worse, and for twelve miles we had to wade through water. . . .

"We reached Brule Lake too late for the train, so we at once started for Canoe Lake Station, where we took a late train into headquarters. Superintendent Bartlett had been successful in taking his party through sections of the park which were off the usual trails and routes, and he had done it under trying conditions at the very worst time of the year. . . . A large amount of information had been gathered regarding timber, game, and routes. . . . We had passed through miles on miles of fine young pine stretching away eastward far beyond the limits of the park. It occurred to us that surely there was a chance for the Department of Reforestization [sic] to put its principles into practice. In years to come, with proper protection, this vast forest of young pine will be worth millions of dollars to the people of Ontario."

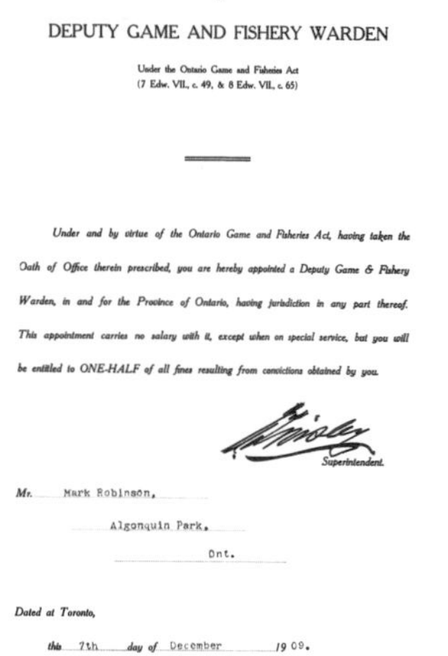

APPOINTMENT TO OFFICE

OF

DEPUTY GAME AND FISHERY WARDEN

Under the Ontario Game and Fisheries Act
(7 Edw. VII., c. 49, & 8 Edw. VII., c. 65)

Under and by virtue of the Ontario Game and Fisheries Act, having taken the Oath of Office therein prescribed, you are hereby appointed a Deputy Game & Fishery Warden, in and for the Province of Ontario, having jurisdiction in any part thereof. This appointment carries no salary with it, except when on special service, but you will be entitled to ONE-HALF of all fines resulting from convictions obtained by you.

Superintendent.

Mr. Mark Robinson,
Algonquin Park,
Ont.

Dated at Toronto,
this 7th *day of* December *19*09.

During the epic winter patrol trip across the Park in 1910, G. W. Bartlett realized that there were not enough well-built shelter lodges in the Park. As soon as spring arrived six new shelters were built and thirteen more huts were constructed during the next two years. By 1936 there was a total of one hundred and fifteen well-built shelter houses.

Once Superintendent MacDougall began making daily winter patrol trips, by plane, the shelter houses were not used as much by the rangers. Two new problems arose: several people who had some connection with higher government officials in Toronto asked for permission to use a ranger's shelter for a vacation; sometimes canoe-trippers broke into a hut during inclement weather, not only leaving it dirty but often breaking up shelves, tables and benches for fire-wood.

By 1950 the Department of Lands and Forests decided to destroy any hut that was not essential. Another era had passed.

A major part of the rangers' work was preventing poachers from trapping in the Park. Many pre-Park trappers thought nothing about making repeated forages into the Reserve. Bartlett reacted forcibly to Archie Belaney's (Grey Owl) boast that he could travel through the Park without encountering a single ranger.

Destroying a ranger house no longer needed.

The story of this attempt was written in *Algonquin Story* and it states that Mark Robinson nursed Belaney for three weeks; another article mentions that G. W. Bartlett obtained two beef galls from the butcher at Whitney and that these were wrapped around Belaney's swollen feet to reduce the pain. Just to clear up any misconceptions, Mark Robinson had made the following entries in his 1909 diary:

"March 15th—Received a letter from Mr. Bartlett regarding a certain Mr. Belaney who was entering the Park from the south. We (Zeph Nadon and Mark) were ordered to go to Moose Lake through to the North River (Oxtongue).

"March 18th—After travelling for three days without seeing any trace of Belaney—We arrived at the Canoe Lake berth in bad shape. Soon after, Bud Callighen and Albere Ranger arrived with Archie Belaney. Zeph and I accompanied them to Headquarters where we stayed for the night.

"March 19th—Got orders to take prisoner to Canoe Lake and feed him, etc.

"March 20th—Mr. Belaney used up in the feet with frost. Decided to keep him until Monday.

"March 22nd—Left this morning to take Mr. Belaney out of our 'beat'. I went as far as Brule Lake and he going as far as Rainy Lake.

Archie Belaney, right, the future Grey Owl, about 1920.

SALE OF FURS FROM ALGONQUIN PARK.

About 400 beaver, and a few mink, marten and otter skins, taken in Algonquin Provincial Park during the past season, by authority of Order-in-Council, will be offered for sale by tender receivable up to four o'clock p.m., Thursday, 1st. June 1916.

The furs will be put up in suitable lots, and bids may be made per lot or per skin, or for the entire quantity. There will probably be a few pounds of castoreum which will be a separate lot.

Terms net cash: one-quarter of the amount offered to be enclosed with tender. The highest or any tender not necessarily accepted.

The furs will be on view at the Parliament Buildings, Toronto, on the 30th. and 31st inst.,

Tenders to be addressed to the Deputy Minister of Mines, and the envelopes containing the same should be marked on the outside "Tender for Furs."

Thos. W. Gibson,
Deputy Minister of Mines.

Toronto, 22nd. May, 1916.

Robinson makes reference to Belaney's ability to tell a good story and made the comment that Belaney had kept them well entertained.

In 1912 a neighbouring local newspaper severely criticized the methods used by the Park staff in their attempt to apprehend poachers. One article went so far as to indicate that trappers could get off the train with their traps and packs and proceed to their "chosen territory" without the knowledge of the rangers. To counter this accusation, George Bartlett ordered all rangers who were near the railway to meet the trains and to enquire from each new arrival about their reason for entering the Park. Since a lot of time was wasted walking the two miles from the Canoe Lake "berth" to the railway station, the subheadquarters was sold to Hugh Trainor, foreman for the Huntsville Lumber Company, for one hundred dollars and the new one re-located at Joe Lake, directly across the bay from the station.

The day Tom Thomson arrived at Canoe Lake Station, Mark Robinson had been tipped off that a poacher was expected to arrive. Thomson was the only stranger with a packsack getting off the train and Robinson, as well as getting particulars of his occupation, intentions, etc., asked him to open his pack for inspection. Thomson complied willingly. After the contents had been checked, Robinson explained why the request had been necessary. From that day on the two were the best of friends.

There had never been enough money from timber dues to finance the Park operations entirely. Since there seemed to be a surplus of fur-bearing animals, it was decided that controlled trapping by the staff would increase the revenue. Beav-

Superintendent Bartlett, Jim Bartlett and Mark Robinson with assorted pelts at Joe Lake shelter house.

er, especially, were too numerous; something had to be done to deplete the population or the animals' health would suffer with the rapid depletion of their main food supplies.[4]

The total revenue from the sale of furs in 1911 amounted to three thousand dollars. Unfortunately it took a great deal of time for the rangers to check their traps, skin the animals, and stretch the hides. This meant less time for patrolling. Regrettably it resulted in a rather unfortunate consequence. Former poachers decided that if the rangers trapped in the Park, they could also. To make matters even worse, some of the rangers got into the fur-selling business for their own profit. One ranger's diary stated, "Must tell my ranger-partner again that his poaching must stop."[5] Over the years there has been more than one ranger fired because of selling furs.

Ranger Jim Sawyer stretching a skin on an alder frame.

Before the Canadian Northern Railway was completed the rangers stationed along the Petawawa waterway had a long distance to travel to get their furs to headquarters. South River, on the Grank Trunk Railway, was the nearest station. One spring it took four rangers in two canoes five days to travel from Cedar Lake to the railroad. Their baggage consisted of 205 beaver skins, 5 mink, 7 marten, 12 muskrats and one fisher—all trapped during the winter of 1910-1911.

Staff trapping in Algonquin Park was discontinued in 1920. Bartlett's 1919 annual report states, "Very little poaching." In Mark Robinson's 1923 superintendent's report he mentions, "There is the usual amount of illegal trapping.... Six offenders were brought in and fines were imposed amounting to $357.45. One hundred and nine traps were brought in with possibly as many more destroyed and a quantity of raw furs were taken for the Department to dispose of at Toronto.

"There is two hundred and fifty-five miles of Park border to guard and one hundred and twenty miles of railroad to watch for poachers. With a staff of thirty-five men it is next to impossible to do the job properly." The ruling that a poacher could not be reprimanded if he managed to escape one mile outside the Park boundary made the task an even harder one.

Poaching continued to be one of the main concerns of the staff until air patrol started in the winter of 1932. Also, at that time, the trappers were organized and each given a registered trapping zone which diminished poaching in the Park greatly.

The early ranger staff wore very tough, rough-and-ready bush clothes, often topped off with a vest and suit coat. "Larrigans" (high laced leather boots) were the most durable shoes for woods travelling. When a ranger met a train, he did not look much like a Park official and a stranger would have no idea that a member of the staff was even present. In 1929 a blue uniform was supplied to chief rangers and deputy-chiefs,

Mark Robinson and son at Joe Lake Station. Bush clothes were considered adequate when meeting trains in 1915.

Mark Robinson in his Chief Ranger's uniform in 1930. It was hardly ever worn.

but these were almost as nondescript as the bush clothes. It wasn't until the mid 1940s that the present khaki uniforms were worn.

One of the Crown Lands' early suggestions had been that, since there was no hotel accommodation, it might be a courtesy to make a shelter hut available to people who were visiting the Park. This policy continued long after there were hotels for tourists. Also, quite often, a ranger was asked to leave his "beat" and take a tourist for a canoe trip.

If a visitor was particularly interested in natural science, either Steve Waters or Mark Robinson would be singled out to be the guide. Waters was known as "Mulvaney" and it was said that he knew the habits of the animals so well that he could have written a Canadian jungle book. Robinson was the "Gineral" because he was supposedly as tall, as thin, and as straight as General Brock's monument at Niagara-on-the-Lake. He had been a military man from the age of twenty-one, and in twenty-five years, he didn't miss attending a June militia camp.

Both these men were spell-binders when telling true woods' experiences. Robinson wrote his first story for *Saturday Night* in 1909, using "Gineral" as a pseudonym. Later articles about the Algonquin area were signed "Mark Robinson, Park Ranger."

Robinson was the guide in 1910 for Joseph Adams, an Englishman who was visiting Canada. After Adams returned to England he wrote *Ten Thousand Miles through Canada*. He says: "To enjoy the real delights of Algonquin Park it is advisable to plan a camping-out expedition. . . . I was fortunate in securing as a guide one of the official rangers, an excellent man, well acquainted with the forests." Adams goes on to say: "Mark, I watch your face as you narrate many a thrilling adventure. I see you turning out and lying on the hard ground to give shelter to the two drenched tourists swamped in their camp on the night of the terrific thunderstorm. I call to mind other things that had upon them the milling and stamping of nature's gentleman."

A ranger had a multitude of other duties thrust upon him, even to settling women's squabbles. There had been more than one "pitched battle" amongst the section-men's wives at Canoe Lake Station in 1912. After repeated efforts to persuade the women to keep the peace, the ranger could see no alternative other than to recommend that all the families be re-located.

One very sad official duty that rangers Robinson and Balfour had to perform was arranging for a doctor to come to the Hayhurst summer cottage on Canoe Lake. More than one member of the family had been ill with diphtheria and one of the boys died on July 12, 1915. Immediate burial in the Mowat

The Hayhurst funeral, 1915, one of the three recorded burials in Mowat cemetery. Mark Robinson rowed the casket over to the Mowat shore. Here he approaches the dock while the father and another ranger look on. The shoreline in this picture is still cluttered with the aftermath of lumbering.

cemetery took place the same day. It had been said that there were several buried in the vicinity of the actual cemetery but there was only the one marked grave, dated 1897. The Hayhurst grave is still the only one identified by the regulation-type headstone.

Another problem for the rangers was to help the lumber company's foreman keep liquor from getting into the camps. The loggers' work was too exacting and arduous to have it disrupted. A catastrophe had occurred on Cedar Lake when nine drunken lumbermen decided to start down the lake in a pointer to go to work and failed to notice that the sluice gate was open. The boat rushed through, drowning all nine. A tall white cross still stands inside a logging-chain fence not far from the Brent millyard.

In the spring of 1908 one lumber company contacted rangers Robinson and Bartlett and said it was rumoured that liquor was to arrive at Canoe Lake station in a five gallon coal oil can and asked them to check the freight carefully. Three cans were taken from the train. Two were checked, and they both contained kerosene. On second thought, the two rangers decided to take a ride on the lumber sleigh and re-check the cans at the depot. Just before reaching the camp Robinson dropped off, saying that he wished to patrol a nearby area. While Bartlett was having lunch with the loggers, Mark circled around and re-checked the cans. Sure enough, one contained whiskey. The snow on the slopes had begun to melt enough to form small rivulets of water so Robinson emptied the whiskey and re-filled the can with water.

After lunch the loggers came tumbling out, each with a cup, to sample the beverage. Imagine their disgust when it was discovered to be only water! There was a lot of talk and some laughter over the incident. The lumbermen blamed the trainmen but couldn't lodge a complaint, while among the ranger staff, all was silence![6]

One evening during the autumn of 1909 Thomas Manion, the pump-house man at Canoe Lake Station, walked the two miles down to Mowat to the subheadquarters to deliver a special letter to Robinson from Superintendent Bartlett. The letter stated that a shooting affair had taken place at Barnet's Misty Lake lumber camp and that he was to proceed at once to arrest a Mr. Hugget who had done the shooting. When Robinson arrived at the Canoe Lake Station to catch the six a. m. train the next morning, the wildest stories were being circulated by the train crew. By the time the train arrived at Brule Lake station the trainmen were quite convinced that Robinson would be the next victim.

First, Robinson went to see Mr. Barnet and was told that the shooting had taken place the day before, Sunday, at two p.m. The wounded man had lived for several hours—just long enough for the priest to be brought in to administer the last rites. The victim exonerated the man who had shot him. He said he had been out setting traps (illegally), heard someone coming, and jumped into a low clump of yew to hide. The "murderer" had shot at the movement, thinking it was an animal. When he had realized his error, he had helped the wounded man back to the shanty.

About three miles along the tote road, Robinson met a man carrying a pack on his back. They both stopped and the other man said, "I suppose you are looking for me; yes, I did kill a man." Robinson asked for his revolver and also requested that he be allowed to inspect his packsack. Robinson found a second revolver and a knife which he confiscated. The "killer" closed his bag, consented to being put under arrest, and asked if a prisoner was supposed to carry his own pack. The answer was yes!

After hearing the circumstances, Bartlett sent a telegram on the following day with instructions to set the man free but to keep the confiscated weapons. The man said, "Well, ranger, thank you. I am through with all this wild life." Robinson had his reservations about that.[7]

The Officers' Co-Reserve List was not called up until the fall of 1915 and Harry (Budd) Callighen and Mark Robinson were given leave of absence from the Park staff for the duration of World War I. However, Robinson was discharged because of a war injury with the rank of Major in April 1917. Callighen did not return to the Park until February 1919, by which time he had earned the rank of Lieutenant.

Bartlett continued to administer Park affairs until his retirement in January 1922. He had served as superintendent for twenty-four years. It has been said that "G. W." saw himself as a defender of the lumber interests. Right or wrong, he was an organized and hard-working man who expected his rangers to be the same. During his regime, it was thought the Park could be self-sustaining. Fishing licenses were sold both to bring in revenue and to ascertain the number of people fishing and the number of fish caught. Staff trapping was to have been the second main financial source (timber dues were first) to provide funds to help finance the Park operations, but it was discontinued in 1920. As a result, the twenties were very lean years with no extra money to hire more staff.

J. W. Millar was sent up from Toronto as acting superintendent from February to October. During this and a later tenure he enlarged the maple syrup operation on the Minnesing road about three miles from headquarters. Unfortunately the peak maple sap-running season coincided with the busiest time, when the rangers were patrolling for poachers. The yield was not high nor the profit sufficiently rewarding to continue the operation after 1942.

Mark Robinson was appointed acting superintendent in October 1922. Although Robinson maintained that the superintendent should be a graduate forest engineer, he was made superintendent the following month.

The ranger staff at Park headquarters at the time of G. W. Bartlett's retirement. Bartlett is second from left.

Even before Bartlett retired, he was fully aware of a well-organized poaching ring but he did not have enough evidence to break it. By the winter of 1924, Robinson was watching for positive proof but the ring was being equally careful not to put any furs on the train while Robinson was around. The Department of Lands and Forests decided that the best way to handle the situation was to give Robinson a leave of absence for three months and then the ring might become careless and be caught "red-handed." This proved to be the case and the culprits were reprimanded.

Because of an illness, resulting in surgery, Robinson was not able to return to the Park staff in 1924. It was more than a year later, in November 1925, that Robinson's doctor gave him permission to return to his Park duties as long as he did outdoor work. He was assigned to the Brent area and, with some extra staff, brought several poachers to court for illicit trapping.

J. W. Millar returned to the Park as acting superintendent and superintendent until 1930. Finally on September 1, 1930, a professional forest engineer, J. H. McDonald, was appointed superintendent. McDonald accepted the post but with the proviso that Mark Robinson be transferred back to headquarters as assistant to the superintendent. McDonald felt he would need his invaluable experience and advice, and although Robinson thoroughly enjoyed his work in north Algonquin, he was willing to work wherever he would be most useful.

Although he was only in his early forties, McDonald died very suddenly of a heart attack in January 1931. Robinson was asked if he would take on the duties of superintendent, but he declined. However, once again he filled in as acting superintendent until F.A. MacDougall was appointed in May 1931. Robinson continued as an adviser until he retired in 1936.

After Frank MacDougall became Deputy Minister of Lands and Forests in 1941, the following superintendents have been in charge: J. M. Taylor (1941-43); George Phillips (1943-58); R. C. Passmore (1959-61); Urho W. "Yorky" Fiskar (1962-65) and T. W. Hueston.

Over the years, the administration of Algonquin Park has not been an easy task. It has often been in the forefront of the news and sometimes has been severely criticized. With the increasing need for wilderness areas and the insatiable demand for more recreational land, the task will not become easier.

Protecting the Forest

Forest protection is concerned with the prevention and control of all elements which cause damage to the forest—fire, disease, insects, unfavourable atmospheric conditions and man's carelessness. Fire will be our main concern in this chapter since forest disease and pests are referred to in a later chapter.

Over the years there have been many huge forest fires that probably became ignited during severe electrical storms. Champlain mentions travelling through "brules" and later explorers noted that vast timber areas had been devastated by fire. Dr. Robert Bell, a geographer, says:

"When the fire has got under way the pitchy trees burn with almost explosive rapidity. The flames rush through their branches and high above their tops with a terrifying sound. The ascending heat soon develops a strong breeze, if a wind does not happen to be blowing already. . . . Great sheets of flame disconnect themselves from the fiery avalanche and leap upwards as towering tongues of fire, or dart forward bridging over wide spaces, such as lakes and rivers, starting fires afresh in advance of the main column. . . . The immense shooting flames are probably due to the large quantities of highly inflammable gas evolved by the heat from the pitchy tree tops just in advance of actual combustion."[1]

The Canadian settlers' policy of burning their forested land in preparation for agricultural crops was often disastrous. Occasionally a fire burned out of control and spread into a raging inferno causing destruction to large quantities of mature timber. As early as 1854 timber operators asked the Commissioner of Crown Lands to prohibit squatters from establishing themselves on Crown Lands. It is questionable whether this request was followed through.

The Superintendent of the Woods and Forests in his 1859 report to the Commissioner of Crown Lands stressed the necessity of taking immediate action for the preservation of the forests from fires. It took twenty-five years before the suggestions in the report became reality. Fire rangers were placed

on Crown Lands under license and the timber companies paid part of the rangers' salaries. Five years later in 1889 fire rangers were appointed to other Crown Lands even though they were not under license.

At the start there was only a skeleton permanent fire ranger staff. The seasonal staff started work on May 1 and, unless the fire hazard remained extremely high, their contract ended on September 30. In the early years the rate of pay was two dollars a day for casual help but by 1910 the rate was

Railway construction in an area ravaged by fires in previous years.

$2.50 a day and the fire ranger paid his own transportation and boarded himself.

Fire rangers worked in pairs on special jobs but a few experienced men sometimes patrolled alone. Each man wrote a daily report and at the end of the season it was turned in to the area headquarters. Fire rangers were constantly on the move, by canoe and on foot, following the railroads, the main waterways and clearing the portages. Copies of the Fire Act were posted in conspicuous places and distributed to settlers, railway workers, timbermen and all others concerned.

Before fire towers were constructed, many a fire-ranger chose his own look-out on a high hill. Some even made a temporary platform at the top of a tall tree. If the summer season was wet a fire-ranger was only reasonably busy but during a dry season there was very little leisure time. Tom Thomson in 1916 found that there was no time for painting. Besides, he found it was impossible to take his sketching kit along. In one of his letters to Dr. MacCallum, Tom said, "One man carries the canoe and the other the packs."

Most of the chief fire-rangers had been bush workers and had had experience in fighting forest fires. It was their job to give new recruits some training at the first of the season and to keep in touch with them during the summer, assisting them when help was needed. The chief fire ranger also had a training session with the loggers, since prompt action on their lim-

A fire-tower in a "look-out" tree at Smoke Lake.

A steel fire-tower.

its could avert a disastrous fire. If a private citizen, the railroad, or construction or timber camps were responsible for a fire, they were charged with the cost of fighting the fire.

How do fire rangers fight fires? There are so many different methods that can be used and each has to be decided on in a split second depending on the type of fire and how far it has gone out of control. Sometimes fire-breaks are made if it is a ground fire that is not moving too quickly; other times, if the wind is in the proper direction, a fire can be headed off towards a lake or swamp; there have been times that it was wise to move the fire-fighters away from the fire to conserve the men's energy until the wind had dropped. Nowadays, if there is a major fire, planes and mechanized equipment are rushed to the scene and experienced fire fighters are brought in from other areas.

The main cause of forest fires is, unfortunately, man and his carelessness; the early wood- and coal-burning railroad engines were a constant hazard; the slash and debris left by the loggers soon dried out and were explosive traps for lightning-induced fires; vast areas of spruce and balsam fir forests, killed by the spruce budworm, were even more dangerous as potential fire hazards than the slash.

In 1912 E. J. Zavitz, the new Director of Forestry in the Department of Lands and Forests and Mines, assumed responsibility for supervising fire protection on the railways in the Province. One of his suggestions to the railroad companies was to keep the right of way well cleared. Before he became an Algonquin guide, Ralph Bice, at the age of fourteen, was one of the casual help who worked at clearing away shrubbery and debris from the embankments between Joe Lake and the Park headquarters. He mentioned that the brush was put in piles to be burned later when the fire hazard was low.

1916 was a very hot, dry summer and there were more large fires than usual across the province. As a result Mr. Zavitz was instructed to reorganize the whole service. The Legislature passed the Forest Fires and Protection Act of 1917 which provided for the new appointment of Zavitz with the title of Provincial Forester. Zavitz was now able to organize all matters pertaining to forest fire prevention, reforestation and tree diseases. With this change of administrative control a separate division, known as the Ontario Forestry Branch, was organized.

J.A. McDonald, a forest engineer, was appointed the District Forester for the Pembroke District in 1922, of which Algonquin Park was a part. Algonquin was divided into two fire-fighting sections: the southern region had its headquarters at Brule Lake and the northern headquarters was at Achray on Grand Lake.

Two regular seasonal fire-fighters, Jim Culhane, left, and Paddy Garvey.

Now that the fire protection was being handled so expertly by the Ontario Forestry Branch, it relieved the Park ranger staff of unexpected interruptions that previously had hampered their work schedule. Mr. McDonald worked closely with Mr. Bartlett and each helped the other's staff as much as possible. The O.F.B. took charge and made the decisions in major fires. If the O.F.B. needed assistance, they asked for it.

The Park staff continued to be just as alert to any fire emergency and often put fires out. One day a frightened porter from a pullman car left on a nearby siding came rushing up to the Joe Lake shelter house shouting, "There's a fire in the spruce swamp through the rock cut!" Robinson moved like lightning. He handed spades to the porter and to his own children, grabbed a pail of water in one hand and an axe in the other. First, Robinson threw water on the ground fire, then, with a couple of well-placed blows with the axe, he felled the burning spruce tree. Everyone shovelled sand over its fiery length until the flames were smothered. The children were all out of breath as they proudly returned to the house with the shovels, pail and axe to report to mother that they had helped fight a fire.

It was very difficult to get fire fighting organized in the years before telephone communication. The trainmen often carried messages, but that was not fast enough. In 1911, G. W. Bartlett was given permission by the Grand Trunk Railway to string a telephone line along the telegraph poles. The same privilege was given along the Canadian Northern once it was completed in 1915. The first bush-line from the Brule Lake chief ranger headquarters to the recently erected steel fire tower at (White) Trout Lake was built in the mid 1920s. A right-of-way was cleared by lopping off the branches from one side of the trees, then the telephone wire was attached. It proved so successful that other lines were gradually installed.

The superintendent's annual report for 1922 states that not only was the Trout Lake tower erected but also a steel tower on the high Skymount hill, at Cache Lake, a third one at the Booth farm, and a wooden tower on the Little Nipissing River. Gradually a whole network of steel towers dotted the Algonquin landscape, with a telephone installed in each tower. (The telephones were later replaced by radios.) At last, messages giving information as to the exact location of a fire could be relayed via the bush line to the nearest fire control station.

Dominion aircraft patrolled the Algonquin area as early as 1921.

A towerman had to be the type of person who did not mind being left alone and who could work quickly when an emergency arose. Some of the men were bush-workers in the winter and others were university students who were glad of a summer's work. The towerman needed to take some training ahead of time since he was required to plot the exact location of a fire on a map with detection instruments. During high fire-hazard periods he worked from dawn to dark but he could take extra time away from the tower during prolonged wet weather. A contented towerman was a person who could draw from his own resources and be happy fishing, photographing, sketching or, best of all, being curious about his wilderness environment. In spite of a few drawbacks connected with the job, he was always glad to be re-hired for another summer and earn the average (1950) pay of five hundred dollars.

In 1925, the Dominion Forest Service in cooperation with the Dominion Meteorological Service started examining the effects of relative humidity and other weather factors on forest fire patterns. The Forest Protection staff was able to use this information to gauge forest fire potential in advance and to warn travellers that the hazard was high and that extra precaution with regard to fires would have to be taken. By 1928 the weather office started giving daily weather forecasts during the fire season.

Forest Travel Permits were first issued in 1929. The traveller was required to outline his full itinerary. It served two purposes: in any emergency that might arise it was an easy matter to check the permits and locate the person; also, if a fire had been left unattended causing a forest fire, the careless person could readily be apprehended.

There was bound to be some duplication of work when both a fire ranger and a park ranger were patrolling the same beat. It was inevitable that the two Algonquin staffs would be amalgamated. When J. H. McDonald was appointed the sixth superintendent of Algonquin Park in August 1930, one of his first duties was to unite the two staffs under the one administration.

If forest fires were to be extinguished speedily, it was essential to have more up-to-date tools to supplement the standard shovel, pick and axe. Portable hand pumps were first used in 1917. More hose was purchased from time to time and in 1922 gasoline powered fire pumps were put into use. By degrees improved equipment had been bought but the depression of the 1930s forced a curtailment in spending.

In *Renewing Nature's Wealth* the Forest Protection reports tell of the effect of these economies by quoting an extract from a 1936 annual report: "1935 Forest Fire Protection—*Equipment* The only major equipment purchased of importance were six new-type pumps. The balance of the purchase was for replacement."[2]

A new threat to the forests emerged during the depression years—arson. Incendiarism, for the purpose of creating new jobs, reached a peak in the summer of 1936. It had been such an extremely dry summer that the forest was tinder dry and that made the fires hard to control. Additional fire-fighting equipment was requisitioned immediately and more staff hired. The weather finally changed and a few days of rain helped the tired staff extinguish the fires.

In 1922 the Ontario Government, in cooperation with the Federal Air Board, started to do some experimental work in forest fire detection, using HS_2L type aircraft. One of the airbases was situated at Whitney, near the Park boundary. Robinson's diary of that summer mentions that the "fire" plane had been making daily inspection trips. When a fire was detected the aerial patrol sometimes put the information in a bag and dropped it near a control station. More often, if near a telephone, the pilot landed the plane and relayed the information.

The experiment, which was carried out in Muskoka and Parry Sound districts as well as Algonquin, proved to the Forest Protection Branch that fire patrol detection planes were practical.

As a result of this report the Department of Lands and Forests appointed a forest engineer-pilot as the seventh superintendent. Frank MacDougall arrived at Algonquin Park with his plane in May 1931. A hangar was built on the shore of Cache Lake behind the headquarters. It was a new experience for the cottagers to listen to the roar of the plane taking off at all hours.

Monty Baker, who had joined the Air Patrol Division in 1924, built the first effective short wave transmitter and receiver set. It was used to code fire information that same summer in the Sudbury district. This was a "first" for an air-to-ground radio in Ontario. Later Baker, with another staff member, built and tested the equipment for ground receiving stations. When Frank MacDougall's Fairchild K-R 34 seaplane arrived at Algonquin it contained an improved transmitting and receiver set. The equipment was large, which made it difficult to operate in the small plane, but MacDougall used it on several occasions.

Later, Baker and his assistants extended their experiments towards developing radios suitable for use at lookout towers. This was a big step toward faster communication to and from the control stations.

In 1932 MacDougall started daily winter inspection trips. These flights were a great help to the Park rangers in capturing and reprimanding members of a large poaching ring.

An Otter water-bomber in action.

The Park's second plane was a five-passenger Stinson S.R.9. It was very easy to use the transmitting-receiving set in the bigger plane. The decision to move the air-base to the less populated and larger Smoke Lake was a good one and in 1939 the present, bigger hangar was built.[3]

From the early days of the air service the Forest Protection staff had been hoping that aircraft would be used extensively in direct fire-suppression work. Experimental dropping of water from aircraft began in 1945. Since then new methods have been perfected and are in constant use in combating forest fires.

One of MacDougall's first concerns after he was appointed Deputy Minister of Lands and Forests in 1941 was to reorganize the whole Department. More staff was put on a full-time basis in the forest protection branch. During the winter portable radios were checked, mechanized machinery made ready, water-pumps given a final over-haul and many talks on protecting our forests were given to schools and public meetings. Once the seasonal staff arrived in the spring there was more time for a thorough training and instruction course.

The permanent protection staff also keeps the bush roads in good repair to ensure that equipment can be moved quickly to the scene of a fire. Taking everything into account it is no wonder that Ontario, and especially Algonquin, is no longer plagued by the fear that forest fires will burn out of control.

The safety record of the Algonquin Air Service has been

excellent considering the many thousand miles of flying that it has done in the more than forty years of service.

It is gratifying to know that Algonquin's first forester-pilot-superintendent, Frank MacDougall, received the McKee Trans-Canada Trophy in 1964 for distinctive achievement as a pilot.

The aftermath of a burn. Five to eight years later, young birch and poplar are growing up.

Wilderness Lodges and Camps

One function for Algonquin Park, as outlined by the Royal Commission in 1893, was not fulfilled until after 1905. It stated that provision should be made in the Park for those seeking not only recreation, but also improved health. The report further mentioned that the inhabitants of Ontario "are still apt to go to Europe or to the United States for health and recreation without trying to find out whether the Northern Ontario air wouldn't be just as beneficial and invigorating."

The railroad officials who came in to check the progress of the railway construction were attracted to the beauty of the Algonquin wilderness.[1] Some brought their families to camp in tents, cook their own meals and generally have fun roughing it. Others took out leases on the lake and erected cottages. The family of Dr. William Bell from Ottawa was one of the first families to build a cottage in 1900 for health reasons.

Mollie Cox, a nurse from Ottawa, came to the Bell cottage in 1900 to improve her health. Once she began to feel better, she made enquiries as to the possibility of obtaining work. Mr. Bartlett suggested that she try cooking for the ranger staff, and Mollie accepted. She proved to be such an excellent cook that it wasn't long before the railroad inspectors asked if they could get some meals at the boarding-house. Later, a few of the "tenters" (mostly families of the railroad officials) requested the same privilege. Mollie Cox could not cope with such an influx of extra visitors and suggested that there was a need for a hotel. The Canadian Railway News agreed to finance the project and the construction was started in 1906. At the same time a permanent Algonquin Park Station was erected. Both buildings were opened officially in July 1908.

Edwin Colson of Guelph joined the Park staff in 1905, met Mollie, and they were married two years later. The Colsons were appointed the first proprietors of The Highland Inn. They continued to look after the hotel until 1913—no easy task since two wings were added during that time.

The first central winterized section of the Inn contained only ten bedrooms, which was not sufficient to meet the tourist demand even for the first year. The management erected several platforms and used tents for the "overflow."

Headquarters at Cache Lake in 1900. Mollie Cox Colson is one of the ladies and possibly the other is Mrs. Bell. Superintendent G. W. Bartlett is the well dressed man on the left, with former superintendent Simpson to his left.

Lizzie Dennison in her Algonquin Hotel kitchen. It was remarkable that she could cook for so many with so few utensils.

The right wing was opened in 1909. Even then it was not large enough to cope with the demand and it was necessary to build an equally large left wing which was opened in 1910. At last the tents and platforms were discarded. The Inn, with its forest green paint, trimmed with white, was an imposing structure. However, the railroad track, which ran below the hotel and between it and the lake, was a slight drawback. Guests hadn't quite expected to hear noisy trains when they had planned their holiday at a wilderness luxury hotel. But the magnificent view over Cache Lake more than compensated for the sound of trains.

In the earlier years it seemed to be the custom for the men to go off fishing with their sons while the wives and daughters stayed behind at the hotel. Playing cards and chatting with the other guests appear to have been the principal pastime although, later, when the tennis courts were completed at the Highland Inn, many people made use of them.

An August 1908 issue of the *Saturday Night* printed a letter, part of which is quoted:

"I have just returned from ten days' fishing at Algonquin Park and while there we stayed at The Highland Inn. . . . I have travelled almost all over the world and I do not think, with any

The first and only winterized section of the Highland Inn was opened in 1908. This picture also shows the new Algonquin Park Station, opened the same year.

Highland Inn in 1922.

exception, that I ever received better or more courteous attention than at this delightful spot."

The Highland Inn was operated first by the Grand Trunk, then the Canadian National until 1928. After that it was sublet by private people and became a very popular place to spend a winter holiday. After forty years, the grand old hotel began to look old and a little neglected. It was not feasible financially to try and repair it so it was sold to the Department of Lands and

Winter sports were popular at the Highland Inn.

Forests in the mid-fifties and torn down. Another landmark, one with a glorious past, had disappeared but will not soon be forgotten.

The Algonquin Hotel, built by Tom Merrill of Rochester, New York, in 1905, was situated on a hill between the dam and railroad on Joe Lake. It commanded an excellent view over upper Joe Lake. Cedar siding, with the bark still on it, had been used to cover the outside of the building, giving the hotel a very rustic appearance. The tourist accommodation, without any sports offered, was open for six months of the year. It was sold to Edwin Colson in 1917.

The Algonquin was always full to capacity since it was well-known for its excellent meals. Lizzie Dennison, gran-

Highland Inn regatta, about 1925.

daughter of John Dennison, who had cleared land on the north shore of Opeongo in 1881, was the cook. She cooked hearty meals at a lumber camp near Combermere in winter and spent the summer cooking for more fastidious tastes.

The Colsons also ran a well-equipped outfitting store, directed by Aunt Annie Colson. Aunt Annie looked severe but was loved by all. On the few occasions when the hotel ordered ice-cream, Aunt Annie would let the children know in advance. That gave the youngsters first chance to buy some. Never has ice-cream tasted so delicious!

Mr. W. W. Hinton, who was in charge of hotel expansion for the Grand Trunk Railway, planned to build two wilderness lodges, patterned along the line of the ones in the Adirondack Forest. The first one was located on Loon Point on the eastern shore of Smoke Lake which had been cleared in the summer of 1912. One of Tom Thomson's sketches shows this area cleared in readiness for construction. The lodge was named "Nominigan," meaning "among the balsams." It was a quiet wilderness camp, seven miles away from the noisy trains. Usually

The Algonquin Hotel, outfitting store (left) and Joe Lake Station, about 1915. Joe Lake Station was one of the few log stations in Eastern Canada.

Nominigan, about 1918.

The Nominigan-Highland Inn "democrat horse-drawn taxi."

the guests disembarked at Algonquin Park Station and took the "democrat horse-drawn taxi" over a rough corduroy bush road.

In January 1913 five railroad officials snowshoed into Island (now Burnt Island) Lake with Mark Robinson to choose a site for a second wilderness lodge. The site wasn't far from the outlet narrows of the lake. The lodge, known as "Minnesing," was constructed that same summer. The super-

The first truck used to deliver provisions to Minnesing Lodge, in the mid-1920s.

intendent's annual report of 1913 states that the Department of Lands, Forests and Mines received $677.90 for the cedar logs that were used for the main lodge and six individual family houses.

The guests booked for Minnesing had a choice of two routes that they could take. One was by the horse-drawn taxi over a road even rougher and longer—eleven miles—than that to Nominigan. If the guests chose to go by canoe from Joe Lake Station, it was more expensive—a guide had to be hired and a canoe rented.

One of the Robinson family's earliest recollections was watching a party of ladies being carefully assisted into the canoes—no easy task since their voluminous skirts had to be tucked in and then a lot of fussing took place to make sure their wide-brimmed picture hats were firmly tied on—and they were on their way. The canoes were still in sight when a sudden thunder storm deluged them with rain. Alas, all those beautiful clothes must have become a sodden mess. The ladies deserved a lot of credit for not demanding to come back to Joe Lake Station—they had two hours of travelling in wet clothes before they reached Minnesing Camp.

One of the men who had worked at The Highland Inn and sister lodges for several years said he earned $45.00 a month and his board in 1925. He sometimes drove the democrat-taxi and recalled that some passengers preferred to walk part of the way rather than being jolted for the full trip. The fee was one dollar for each passenger. In winter he was a general maintenance man at The Highland Inn. He kept the skating rink clear of snow and flooded the rink each night. Another daily

Minnesing. The interior was decorated with attractive rustic furniture. Note the carbide lamps.

job was to keep a large area of ice free from snow since this would allow the ice to freeze to a greater depth. Ice was harvested from Cache Lake for the hotel, the railroad cars and the headquarters' staff buildings.[2]

It has been said, but not authenticated, that The Highland Inn, with its heavy winter expenses, usually ended the year in the red but that the wilderness lodges that only operated in the summers showed a profit.

The Nominigan cabins burned to the ground in 1926 but the main lodge was saved, and Garfield Northway, a Toronto businessman, bought it in 1931 from the Canadian National Railways. Nominigan, as a luxury wilderness lodge, was ended.

In 1923, Dr. Henry Sherman, a retired California scientist,

bought Minnesing Camp for the purpose of holding seminars to study the life of Jesus. People came from all walks of life, had a relaxed holiday, and left with renewed faith. This unique camp continued until the early 1940s.

Mowat Lodge (named Camp Mowat for its first year of operation) was opened for business in the late summer of 1913 by Shannon and Annie Fraser. R.P. Little, who had spent many months in the Park regaining his health, says he was Mowat's first paying guest in September. Tom Thomson and H.B. Jackson arrived in the Park in May 1912 for a canoe trip. Shannon Fraser watched them load their canoe at the Mowat dock in the teeth of a high wind and suggested it might be wise to stay overnight with him. There may have been other unofficial guests before Fraser got around to advertising his place as a fishing lodge in 1913.

As previously mentioned, the Lodge had been a mill boarding-house. Fraser had been postmaster at Mowat and continued running the post office after the Lodge was opened for business.

Camp Mowat was a financial success in its first year. This could have been due to Annie Fraser's excellent cooking and the casual atmosphere that she created. It certainly couldn't be credited to the beauty of the surroundings because the slabs of wood, sawdust and other mill rubbish could still be seen. No wonder it has been next to impossible to find any

Mowat Lodge in winter 1917.

photographs—no one wanted to take a picture of such barrenness.

Fraser advertised his lodge as being open all year and stressed the "health-compelling climate." The rates were moderately priced, which meant that people suffering from a prolonged illness could afford to stay there.

Mowat's brochure was the only one that suggested that campers could arrange to come for regular meals. It stated, "On Canoe Lake are any number of unsurpassed campsites, where parties can set up their tents and still be in touch with mail . . . source of supplies . . . taking one or two meals each day at the hotel, if desired."

The lodge could have been continuously successful if it had been managed in a more business-like way. Annie was too busy to have time and Shannon too often put showmanship before practical essentials. For instance, he wanted a fire-place in the "lobby" but Annie said they could not afford it. Fraser, not to be out-done, had a new brochure printed and included the following: "The hotel provides the added relaxation and pleasure of sitting before an open fire-place in the evenings."[3] Fraser got his fire-place! And where he got the idea of buying a horse-drawn coach from an undertaker—nobody knows. There is no doubt that Fraser looked very impressive driving the coach to the station to meet in-coming guests. The Canoe Lake young people called it "the hearse" and gave Fraser the unofficial title of Mayor of Mowat.

The first Mowat Lodge burned to the ground in November 1920 while Mrs. Fraser and daughter, Mildred, were away. Very little furniture or clothing were saved but the livestock and fowl were rescued. The Frasers paid George Rowe one thousand dollars in cash for his neat little cottage which had

A swimming party near Mowat, 1919.

The new Mowat Lodge, about 1924. It was built on the site of the old Gilmour mill. To the far left is the Blecher house, next the square original Gilmour office building, and the Trainor cottage, previously the Canoe Lake Berth and before that "the Manse."

been built adjacent to the old Gilmour mill foundation two years before.[4] This became their permanent home. Immediate plans were made to re-build but this time the location was changed and the lodge was erected on the footings of the old Gilmour mill. This site was an improvement because the chipyard was behind the building, and the guests could now sit on the veranda and gaze across Canoe Lake. The first section was completed in time for the 1921 tourist season.

Shannon Fraser must have decided to be up to date because he discarded his horse-drawn coach and bought a Model-T Ford. The car didn't have the prestige that the coach had but it was much more useful.

Nina Millen, a guest, tells about one trip she took in the Model-T: On the way from the station to the lodge a cow stood in the middle of the road. No amount of honking would make it move. Finally, Shannon bunted the cow and jolted her into the ditch. Miss Millen protested such tactics and said, "What if you had harmed her?" Fraser's answer was typical of him: "It doesn't matter, she belongs to me."[5] Mowat kept their own cows to supply the hotel with milk. It has been said that Fraser always wore a dress shirt and tie, as well as his fedora, when he milked the cows.[6]

In May 1930 Mowat Lodge, as well as the adjoining cottage, burned to the ground. This time Fraser did not have the heart to re-build and the family moved to Kearney and later to Huntsville.

Larry (Lowrie) Dixon and George Rowe had been at Canoe Lake since the very early 1900s. Dixon was a general handyman and did some guiding. Rowe was an excellent guide and at other times he worked for Fraser—that is when he and Dix-

Shannon Fraser with his horse-drawn coach.

on were not being fired. Both Dixon and Rowe had an alcoholic problem that occasionally interfered with their work. They lived together for many years in one of the Gilmour shacks and it was this house that Arthur Lismer sketched and titled, "The Artist's Hut." Later, Ranger Balfour helped Dixon build a new house near the conjunction of Joe and Potter creeks. Their friendship came to a sudden and tragic end. Rowe and Dixon were paddling up the creek to Dixon's cabin in the midst of a stormy April night in 1918. Their canoe hit a "deadhead" (submerged log left from the timber days) and flipped both men into the freezing water. Dixon landed on a sharp protrusion attached to a stump and it pierced one lung. Rowe clung to another stump, shouting for help.

Was it possible that Mollie Colson could have heard Rowe calling from over a mile away? Mollie was a nurse who had developed an almost uncanny sensitivity to the needs of a patient. She must have possessed some extra-sensory perception which enabled her to be positive that she could indeed hear someone calling for help. She convinced her husband, Ed, that they must go at once to the bottom of Joe Creek. They rescued Rowe and Dixon just in time. Both men were almost completely exhausted from the ice-cold water. Dixon did not respond to treatment and preparations were made for Mollie to accompany him to the Toronto General Hospital where he died two days later (May 4th).

Rowe was so grateful to the Colsons for saving his life that he decided to work at the Algonquin Hotel rather than at Mowat. He built another cottage between Joe Lake dam and the Algonquin Hotel and spent the rest of his life in this new location.

When G. W. Bartlett retired in 1922 the post office was moved from headquarters to the Highland Inn outfitting store, making it more convenient for the tourists to get their mail while shopping for supplies. The post office had lost all its former splendour. It was now tucked away into a far corner as if it were unimportant. Alfred Bartlett had always looked friendly and kindly and seemed to be interested in solving people's postal problems. Also the ornate brass bars on the wicket-window at the former location made children, especially, feel it was a very important place.

Alf Bartlett bought the Dr. William Bell cottage across the lake, erected more buildings and opened it up as a tourist resort in 1923 under the name Bartlett Lodge. It is still operating after fifty years of continuous service.

The buildings of Opeongo Lodge had once belonged to the St. Anthony Lumber Company when they had had a depot there. Sandy Haggart bought the buildings in 1932 and rented a couple of cottages as well as keeping the lodge open for guests. Later he sold the property to J. E. Avery of Whitney.

The hotel is no longer in operation but there is a well-equipped outfitting store, still run by the Averys and doing a big business there today.

Kish Kaduk Lodge on Cedar Lake has been open since 1928. It has always been operated by the Thomas family and Jack Wilkinson. It has been a very successful business but now it is an outfitting outlet only, with a couple of housekeeping cabins available.

Whitefish Lodge, on Lake of Two Rivers, was another tourist centre that had reached such a state of disrepair that it seemed advisable to sell it back to the government.

The Wigwam Lodge at Kiosk and the Lake Traverse Camp were both situated on the Petawawa water route. They were close enough to Montreal and Ottawa to entice many an ardent fisherman.

The Red Gods Camp on Buck (Tepee) Lake had been planned by Ernest Thompson Seton and Ellsworth Jaeger in 1931 as an art and craft camp. Unfortunately it opened at the beginning of the Depression and was forced to close in 1934. Mrs. M. Kates bought it and in 1935 opened it as Camp Arowhon. It was the only camp in the park where the boys and girls shared the same site and activities. Mrs. Kates built Arowhon Pines on a neighbouring lake and it is still in operation. Originally it was built for the parents of the campers but now caters to other adult groups as well.

Since 1935 Killarney Lodge on Lake of Two Rivers has been and still is one of the best tourist lodges in the Muskoka and Haliburton districts.

At Ahmek the sandy beach was littered with uprooted pine stumps and drowned trees that had drifted in. Each evening the campers cleared a part of the beach and built a huge bonfire. In this picture the uncleared part of the beach can be seen in the background.

There are many permanent young people's camps in Algonquin Park. Arowhon has already been mentioned. The first camp in Algonquin was Waubeno for boys and was established on Cache Lake in 1908. Northway Lodge for girls was started on Cache Lake in the summer of 1909.

All the early boys' camps, including Waubeno, were offshoots of American military academies: Pathfinder, on Source Lake is still operating; the Long Trail Camp on upper Joe Lake was terminated by World War I; Camp Minnewawa on Lake of Two Rivers started in 1911 and closed in 1930; Camp Ahmeek, on Lady Joe Lake, from 1911-1922 (this site is now used by Arowhon Pines as a recreation centre for the children of their guests).

Camp Tamakwa is an American boys' camp, established in 1937. It can been seen from the highway on the far shore of South Tea Lake.

The Taylor Statten Camps on Canoe Lake have become known all over North America. They have always been leaders in new approaches to camp organization. The boys' camp, Ahmek, was opened in 1921 and the girls' camp, Wapomeo, in 1924.

Camp Tanamakoon, an excellent camp for girls and Canadian like Arowhon and the Taylor Statten camps, was organized in 1925 by Mary Hamilton, principal of Margaret Eaton School in Toronto.

During the Second World War the boys and girls of some of the camps carried on as assistants to the reduced ranging staff. Groups from the camps helped to clear portages, built landing docks at the end of portages and even made some fireplaces, tables and a few shelters at campsites. The De-

Objibway Indians teaching birch-bark canoe building.

Taylor Statten inspects a wilderness cabin built by boys from Ahmek.

partment of Lands and Forests supplied the materials and Mr. Maurice Kirkland was the coordinator. Some of the senior boys outlined a new canoe route and cut out new portages through one of the less travelled parts of the Park.

The Junior Forest Ranger program was developed in 1944 on a small scale because the voluntary work done by the older boys and girls at the Algonquin Park private camps had proved how valuable it had been to have seventeen-year-olds work in the bush.

Canoeing and Camping

Poling through the shallows.

James Wilson, Superintendent of Queen Victoria Niagara Falls Park, after travelling through Algonquin, stressed:

"In order to facilitate the movements of the rangers in patrolling the streams and rivers, I would suggest the advisability of the erection of simple timber dams at points where there are small rapids and shallows so as to reduce the length of the portages to a minimum.... Every... bit of river that can be navigated by canoe will make the work of the rangers more effective, and at the same time the toil incident to the long portages will be avoided...."

With reference to the extensive lumbering operations, Wilson says:

"This condition of affairs has however some redeeming features, one of these being the improvement of the waterways, by the erection of dams at the outlets of the lakes and at some of the rapids or falls, the effect of which is to raise the level of the water, and also by removing obstructions in the streams and rivers."

In spite of the hardships and frustrations of his first inspection trip, Wilson became quite lyrical about the excellence of the Park waterways for canoeing:

"To the tourist the continual change from lake to river, from river to portage, and from portage to river and lake again, make a delightful panorama which captivates the eye and the senses, and ... impels a seeking after more perfect knowledge of the many varieties of animal and vegetable life which have their habitat in the territory."[1]

The George B. Hayes party of Buffalo planned their first fishing trip into the future Park in 1880. They arranged transportation with different lumber companies and made use of their tote roads to reach the starting point of their trip.[2]

The tourists' views of what constitutes a successful wilderness holiday have changed vastly over the years. Shortly after the turn of the century it was the "thing to do" to plan a fishing trip to Algonquin National Park. An entry in Mark Robinson's 1909 diary says, "Took Joseph Adams fishing at Whiskey Falls on the Oxtongue river; ten other fishermen passed by during the afternoon."

Previous to 1910 there were far more Americans than Canadians visiting Algonquin. One American gave his version as to why his countrymen travelled more: "We have two main objectives to save money for, one is Christmas and the other holidays; we save diligently all year, spend every cent we own (and sometimes more) on a trip to Canada and then return home, well satisfied with the venture but without a cent to our names." Canadians, at that time, seemed too

The Hayes fishing party, 1897. A lumber company wagon brings in supplies.

George B. Hayes, extreme left, meets rangers Tim O'Leary and Steve Waters. The loon skins are being stretched and will be used as liners for their moccasins in winter.

frugal in their spending to dream of putting pleasure before financial security.[3] Thomas Gibson, writing in the October 1899 issue of the *Canadian Magazine* states: "As its (Algonquin's) attractions become better known, they will invite crowds of heated, tired and worried tourists to cheat the dog-days by spending them in the cool depths and silent fastnesses of this northern forest." Even the reasons for a northern holiday have changed vastly!

Before 1920 a guide was considered absolutely essential to a successful fishing trip. Guiding was a lucrative business for the winter woods' worker or trapper.

The Mowat Lodge brochure says:

"All guides have to be approved and licensed by the Park superintendent. As most of these men live some distance from Canoe Lake, and the demand exceeds the supply, those wishing them should write ten days in advance to prevent disappointment. The canoes, tents and outfits are rented from the hotel management which assumes no responsibility as to the guides' charges... though endeavoring to supply only competent and reliable men.... The management acts only as a medium through which they may be hired and derives no profit therefrom."

Each hotel provided a "guide house." The building contained one big room which provided free accommodation for the guides. The men brought their own bedding and ate their meals in the hotel staff dining room. A guide paid for his own meals (usually twenty-five cents) if he was not under contract to a party, otherwise the employers paid the guide's food bill. In 1893, James Wilson paid his guide, who supplied his own canoe, $2.00 a day.[4] Until 1920, a guide earned three dollars a day and, if he used his own canoe, he received an additional fifty cents a day. These rates were increased the next year to four dollars a day and one dollar extra for the guide's canoe. If a junior guide was employed he earned half as much.[5]

The Highland Inn booklet of the thirties quotes fifty-five dollars a week for a guide and equipment such as tent, canoe, blankets, dunnage bags and provisions.

If there had been such an organization as a "closed corporation" it might have been said that the veteran guides had the "inside track." It was quite difficult for university students to break through such an established barrier to obtain any of the long-term jobs. Naturally, returning tourists always asked for their previous year's guide if he had proven satisfactory.

George Rowe stayed near Mowat Lodge and worked as a general handyman and guided during the summer. Before coming to the Park to work at the Gilmour Mill Rowe had won

A newly cut portage in 1897. The Hayes' guides cooking lunch.

A guide portaging supplies.

first prize as a typesetter at the Chicago World's Fair in the 1890s. When questioned about his preference in making Algonquin Park his home he simply answered, "I like it here."

Rowe was in demand—he talked well; he was efficient and patient and did his best to make his "parties" comfortable. Sometimes this was no easy task. A supposedly true incident involves Rowe and a wealthy businessman who was both demanding and belligerent. One stormy day he insisted that Rowe take him across one of the larger lakes to fish. Rowe tried to reason with him and explained that the lake was rough enough to be dangerous. The businessman persisted in

A 1909 fishing party.

his demand to be taken across and Rowe, in exasperation, said, "Nothing doing. If I drown you, I'll lose my license." The wealthy fisherman retorted, "We have life-saving cushions." Finally Rowe relented and said, "Get into the canoe." A few yards from shore, "by accident" Rowe let a huge wave wash into the canoe and the "boss" had to sit in a couple of inches of water. "Go back!" was the frantic cry but Rowe explained that he couldn't turn without dumping the canoe. Rowe paddled expertly but slowly over the wind-tossed waves and as they neared the far shore, again "by accident," the boat overturned. One can imagine, without specific description, how wildly the businessman thrashed about in the water. When Rowe thought his party had had enough punishment, he told him he could touch bottom and walk ashore if he put his feet down. Rowe often told this story, probably with more exaggeration at times, but he always finished it by saying, "Naturally he fired me but I had him well-broken in for the next guide."[6]

Guides are still hired, especially for the early speckled trout fishing. As well, people who are not familiar with wilderness canoeing prefer to have an experienced guide. Guides know how to make a temporary over-night camp comfortable and they seem to know the best places for good fishing.

Bernard Wicksteed, a British author, tells in his book *Joe Lavally and the Paleface* how he had always wanted to go on a canoe trip with an Indian guide. Joe had assured him before starting the trip that he would take him through solitary wilderness where they would not see another canoe from one day's end to another. When they encountered five canoes on the first lake going in the same direction "B. W." asked Joe about it. As usual Joe had a ready answer: "Well sir, when you says this trip is a school boy's dream come true, I didn't reckon on you bringing the rest of the school with you."

Even thirty years ago it wasn't always easy to get a choice campsite. Joe Lavally had a particular site in mind for the first night. He suspected that the cavalcade of canoes was headed for the same place. Each time Joe paddled faster, the others did the same. As they came nearer to the chosen island Joe sped by on the right side as the others canoed towards the left side. Joe triumphantly reached the landing rock mere seconds before the other canoes had rounded the point.

In the chapter on forest protection, the advisability of issuing Forest Travel Permits was discussed. Since 1929 the records of tourists' itineraries have been helpful not only for forest fire control but in other emergencies. Back in the early 1960s, a sixteen-year-old camper became separated from the rest of her party. All tourists travelling anywhere near were notified to join in the searching. In spite of careful patrolling of the area it took more than a day before she was found. How could it happen? The unpredictable human element was the reason that made it hard for the searching parties to decide just where the girl was. This is what had happened. Two parties were travelling the same route but the first one was to keep well ahead of the other. The lost girl belonged to the second group. At one of the portages, she quickly grabbed her packsack and ran over the portage in the hopes of getting across for a chat with a special friend in the first group before they left. In her hurry she kept her eyes on the path and didn't even notice that she had veered onto an old lumber road instead of staying on the portage. After considerable time she began to think she should have reached her destination sooner. She dropped her pack (the first error) and tried to find her way back by going diagonally through the bush rather than retrace her steps. Much later she discovered that she couldn't find either the portage or her pack. Undaunted, she was determined to find her own way. As evening approached she came to a dilapidated old logging building near a stream. She cut boughs from a balsam fir tree and arranged a bed on the roof of the building. She heard faint shouts later in the evening, upstream, but did nothing about answering. She didn't even walk upstream the next morning.

This camper had done a lot of canoe-tripping and thought she knew how to find her way out. Hindsight is easier than foresight. There were so many obvious plans that should have been considered: she should not have left the packsack nor tried to take a short-cut through dense forest; she should have followed the stream until it reached a lake and there she could have been seen readily by the searching planes. It took three days to locate her and this incident happened on one of the busiest canoe routes in Algonquin Park.[7]

To an old-time canoe-tripper the present, over-crowded routes do not provide much of a thrill. Many of them plan a trip "off the beaten track" but no longer can one come upon a deserted logging camp as was possible in the late twenties and be able to picture in his mind what it must have looked like in the active lumbering days. Part of the fun used to be to come upon a deserted camp. The cook-shanty might have an old bean-pot sitting in it and the flooring, or what was left of it, would be chewed up by porcupines because the salt from the pork fat had been spilled and had worked its way into the timbers. At the Perley farm on the Little Nipissing River part of a make-shift fence surrounding the pig-pen area was still standing in the 1930s; the root-house, smelling very dank and partially rotted away, still showed clearly that great care had been taken to keep perishable food, such as potatoes, in good condition for human consumption. At the Booth farm an old

Abandoned depot of the Gillies Lumber Company on the Petawawa River, 1930. The house on the left was used by ranger Zeph Nadon.

Exploring an old lumber camp.

pointer had been pulled up on shore so long ago that three birch trees, about twelve feet tall, had grown up through the rotting floor boards. Another find which made one's mind gallop back into history was an old pine stump with the wire cable still attached—probably used to "winch" or "inch" a lumber company's "alligator" across a portage.

During the mid 1930s, the depression years, the government was urged to create jobs for the unemployed. One of the projects was to clear the rivers of submerged stumps and deadheads and to tidy up the shores of the lakes visited by tourists most frequently. One lady, who returned to Algonquin Park for a holiday after a twenty year absence, thought the shores of the lakes looked unnatural.

A pre-1915 tripper, if he felt energetic, thought nothing of clearing his own campsite, even to building a fire-place and possibly a table if the site wasn't too far from an old lumber camp. And oh, the bliss of making one's own balsam bed! No one thought of conservation in those days.

A tourist on a fishing trip, 1916-style.

The present day canoe-trippers would never plan a trip with the minimum amount of food and equipment that the earlier campers planned. In the 1930s, if one of a party of three owned his own canoe, the cost for a two-week trip, including transportation to and from Toronto, would be approximately one dollar a day for each person. The dollar-and-a-half entrance fee to a provincial park is only the beginning of the present day canoeing holiday.

For a short time after Highway 60 was completed, it began to look as if wilderness camping were on the decline but this is no longer the case. In fact the main water-route from Canoe

Lake to Cedar Lake (total eighty miles) has been nicknamed "Yonge Street." As early as 1967 on a holiday weekend there were ninety-six canoes either waiting to cross or on their way over the Joe Lake portage on a Saturday.[8] There are both shorter and longer trips suggested in the Algonquin Park (Centennial) folder with a map included. This booklet is illustrated with coloured reproductions of Tom Thomson paintings and is worth keeping as a memento of an Algonquin holiday.

Special canoe and paddling instruction is given at Canoe Lake Portage by a summer staff member of the Ministry of Natural Resources. The expert will not only answer some of your questions but will also show you the best way to pack your canoe for the maximum safety.

Sometimes rules are disregarded. In 1929, a party of seven people and three canoes got a travel permit to paddle down the turbulent Petawawa river. They boasted that they intended to shoot all the rapids rather than portage. Fortunately they did not try to shoot the Devil's Chute. However, they did try one rapid too many. Mark Robinson, who was making a hurried trip on a motorized hand-car known as a "jigger" to Lake Traverse, noticed a smashed canoe on the rocks in the Petawawa river below the railroad. Mark rushed down the embankment and saw that a woman was wedged between two rocks. Each time, after the rushing water passed over her, she managed to raise her head high enough to get a breath of air. It was quite a struggle for Mark to get a firm footing in the swift current while he loosened her

Girls at Northway Lodge camp, about 1920.

What not to do. A few canoe parties have lost their gear and taken a soaking trying to shoot rapids that are too swift.

A lazy way to portage, 1916. The crazy wheel between Rock Lake and Long Lake. Abandoned by the lumber company, it was used occasionally by canoe trippers. It no longer exists.

clothing, which was firmly hooked over another rock. Once he got her ashore and knew that she was all right, he dashed down the river to look for the rest of the party. They all had made shore without too much disaster other than getting everything soaking wet. Robinson took them to the next ranger station until a new canoe was shipped from North Bay, when they were able to continue their trip. All in all it was a rather terrifying experience that they vowed they wouldn't want to repeat.[9]

Even before the road through Algonquin was comfortable to travel on, tourists began making individual campsites on the shores of the bordering lakes. This was highly unsatisfactory because it was difficult to supervise so many different campsites. As a result plans were immediately made to have centralized camping locations set up for overnight or longer camping.

This type of camping grew by leaps and bounds until, by 1953, the recreational facilities along the Algonquin highway were inadequate. The Division of Parks was formed in 1954 and one of their policies was that all privately leased properties in the Park would revert to the Crown as the leases expired. On the termination of a lease the "holders" would either sell their buildings to the Crown or donate them to the people. For instance, the Barclay estate at Rock Lake was offered as a convalescent hospital for sick children but it wasn't accepted because the long distance from any city plus the overhead cost of keeping up such a large establishment was prohibitive. The

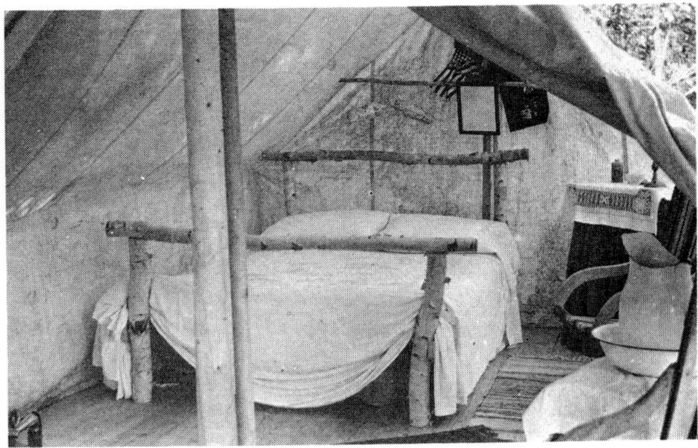

Permanent campsites could be leased for a small sum. A permanent wooden platform would be built on which to pitch the tent. In this luxurious camp in 1915, the cook came along and all the amenities of home were provided.

buildings were taken down and the property has become one of the most picturesque group camping areas in the Park.

Looking back through the eighty years of Algonquin Park's existence, there is no doubt that the tourists have been more orientated to canoe-tripping and fishing than hiking.

This was quite forcibly emphasized by an American family who were discussing different vacations with a Canadian group on top of Mount Katahdin in Maine (northern point of the Appalachian Trail). They were amazed that it was the Canadians' first hiking holiday and that they had never before thought of any other type of holiday than canoe-tripping. The American parents had taken their boys the previous summer to Algonquin Park because it was considered to be one of the trips that all families should take. The ten to fourteen-year-olds

Making a canoe serve two purposes.

felt too captive having to paddle in a canoe so much of the day. The portages were paths that had to be laboured over in a minimum amount of time and not for enjoyment. "Never again," said the Americans.

It just proved that there were two sides to every point of view. Algonquin Park decided to do something about a hiking trail in 1962. The seventeen-mile trail starting at the Lake of Two Rivers Airport has been re-routed to make two trails since the longer length seemed to scare the average tourist away from even starting. It isn't a trail to race over in order to say you have done it. First get the information booklet from the Park Museum. It tells you some of the background history of the area as well as many things to look for. The secret of really enjoying the trail is to do it leisurely, back-packing your food and sleeping bag with no set time to be back. One of the Park policy announcements of July 1973 recommends more travel routes to be established for hiking. This is good news for those who prefer this type of holiday to the usual canoeing vacation.

Enthusiasm for winter camping has been growing steadily. The nearest winter campsite to Algonquin Park is Arrowhead, immediately north of Huntsville on Highway 11. There are heated washrooms, electrical outlets and running water available not far from each campsite. Arrowhead campers

Camping in the 1970s.

plan day trips into Algonquin to observe birds, examine animal tracks, and listen to wolves howling.

In 1970, a team of cross-country skiers, without the knowledge of the Park staff, decided to do a marathon trip from Cedar Lake, following the main water-route they had canoed through the summer before, to the highway at Canoe Lake. The trip took longer than planned because the skiers hadn't foreseen that the faster-flowing rivers would not be frozen over or that the ice at the inlets and outlets of the lakes would not be safe to travel on. Skiing around these danger zones meant climbing up many hills and "bush-whacking" through the woods.

Another winter camping trip by snowshoe in 1963 was very carefully prepared. The chosen camping spot was on the island in Little Island Lake (between Cache and Smoke Lakes). It was a strenuous trip because not only was the ice covered with deep slush but there was a strong head wind and heavy snow falling. The main object of the trip was to attempt to do some under-the-ice photography. Found Lake was chosen because it was known to be a very deep lake in relation to its surface area.

A square hole was cut in the ice and two of the campers, in their "wet-suits" and carrying underwater cameras, plunged into the ice cold water. The third member of the party stayed on the surface and held the guide-lines that were attached to their suits. This was essential because the snow on the surface ice prevented any light from penetrating under-water and the divers could not possibly have found their own way back to the opening. As they had surmised they couldn't see a living creature in such blackness, but at least their curiosity was satisfied.

Winter camping on an experimental expedition. The fire boils water for tea and sheets of aluminium foil reflect heat into the lean-to. Bill and Ed Addison are the cooks.

Divers Ario Gatti and Bill Addison about to submerge beneath the ice.

Forests, Fish and Wildlife

Alexander Kirkwood's report of 1886 gives reasons for setting aside a portion of Ontario as a Park and suggests that the name Algonkin Forest and Park would be appropriate since the name represents one of the greatest Indian nations which has inhabited the North American continent. Kirkwood defined a forest "as a certain territory of woody grounds and fruitful pastures privileged for wild beasts and fowls of the forest.... This forest and its foresters will be the means of protecting them (wildlife) in their habitat.... There will be no hunting therein for pleasure or pastime but fishing in the waters will be allowed."

The ends to be attained were:

> maintenance of water supply, especially of the headwaters of those rivers which have their sources therein; to undertake experiments in forestry; to protect wildlife.

Peter Thomson, the first superintendent, purchased some pine seed and gathered pine cones in the hope of extracting the seed. He also sowed wild rice and wild celery in possible habitats. He carried half a bushel of acorns from Toronto and had them planted in 1894. Thomson even brought some apple trees to the Park in the hope that they might adapt successfully. Even though Thomson's trees did not survive, an apple tree on the duFond farm was still blooming in the 1930s.

John Simpson, Thomson's successor, stated in his 1895 annual report that the experiment of collecting and extracting the seed from the pine cones was unsuccessful. The wild rice and wild celery were also unproductive.

George Bartlett, the third superintendent, planted one hundred trees, mostly sugar maple, in 1902, and in 1908 he had Norway spruce, white spruce and a few pine planted on the headquarters' grounds on Cache Lake. Bartlett suggested that a second attempt be made to establish wild rice and wild celery but this time sow it at lakes where the water level would not fluctuate because of the timber drives. Once again it was a failure. Apparently the ecological requirements for these species were not well known or understood. Today we know that these introductions would never have been successful.

The first "forestry field-practice camp" from the University of Toronto came to Burnt Lake, Algonquin National Park in 1908. Dr. E. B. Fernow, Dean of the Faculty of Forestry, Dr. J. H. White, the Faculty's first graduate, and three students made up the "party." Professor T. W. (Teddy) Dwight, one of the students, still clearly remembers that trip and that the name of the ranger who accompanied them was Bob Balfour.

Professor Dwight recalled that Balfour used a birch bark canoe that was rather skittish. The university party had Chestnut canvas canoes that were more seaworthy. When the party reached Big Trout Lake it was too stormy for the bark canoe and they did not proceed until the wind subsided. The party camped near the shelter house and had their meals with Balfour. One evening as Balfour made bannock for supper they watched the process with great fascination. He went over to the bag of flour, made a hollow, then casually poured a small container of water into the bag. He deftly folded the flour from around the edges into the liquid until the dough could be lifted out without leaving any moisture. The cooked bannock was quite edible when hot but very tasteless and like hardtack when eaten cold.

The group paddled over to the Barnet Lumber Company's depot each day to study lumbering methods. Professor Dwight recounts how well the camp was operated and how much they learned from the skilled timbermen.[1]

Dwight's general impression of the Park was that there seemed to be more emphasis by the local staff and government administrators on wildlife and the prevention of poaching than on forestry.

The Faculty of Forestry field camp did not return to Algonquin Park until 1924. For the next eleven years they used the

The first University of Toronto forestry field camp at Algonquin in 1908. They camped next to Burnt Lake shelter hut on ranger Bob Balfour's beat.

Ontario Forestry Branch buildings at Achray on Grand Lake. The studies also included a visit to the nearby Petawawa Experimental Station. One of the students, Stan Losee, described the beauty of the scenery in this part of Algonquin:

"There is a fine view from the top of a fifty foot cliff overlooking a black spruce swamp. The dark green and regular form of the spruce contrasts strongly with the irregular highly coloured hardwoods which surround it. Although the swamp is level the spruce decreases in height towards the centre where it is wetter and gives a saucer-like effect almost like an amphitheatre."

The interior of the building was not very picturesque.

"It is a rough board shack, the rafters piled high with spare fire-rangers' equipment, shovels, extra beds, paddles and the added touch of the students' town clothes. The walls are lined with double-decked steel bunks which are decorated with more clothes, packsacks, socks and many other odds and ends."[2]

The preliminary plans for silvicultural research were almost completed when the depression of the thirties forced the project to be cancelled. Much later, in 1950, a reserve of mature hardwoods of 2,400 acres was set aside in the vicinity of Swan Lake. A study of the silvics of the main species of the Park is being made with the view to eventual use of the information in future forest management. Sugar maple and yellow birch have been and still are being studied extensively.

Considerable reforestation, especially in the Kiosk and Lake Opeongo regions, was carried out in fire-ravaged areas in the mid 1930s. Lumber companies were also beginning to do some reforesting on their "cut-overs."

Natural regeneration of certain tree species occurs with great rapidity. Birch and poplar grow quickly. One example was observed at Rain Lake after the railroad ties had been lifted from the abandoned railroad line. Balsam fir had grown on one part of the right of way to a height of nine to twelve feet in seven years.

Peter Thomson, in his annual report in 1894, states: "All the lakes are well stocked with fish. Grey or lake trout, salmon and brook trout are the principal kinds found.... Large numbers of the young of these fish are annually destroyed by gulls and loons and it might be advisable to consider the propriety of waging war on the latter, as neither bird is of much commercial value...." If such dire action had been carried through there would have been many to express concern.

There was no doubt that the flooding of the lakes, in preparation for the spring log drives, had a detrimental effect on the fish population. It destroyed not only spawning beds but also specialized feeding areas. To overcome partially this difficulty definite specifications were sent to each timber company operating in Algonquin waters, as to when and for how long the waters could be held back.

1892 was the first year that a creel limit was set in Ontario and naturally the same rule held for Algonquin Park. It was always necessary for fishermen to buy a license in the Park until the spring of 1971 when all fishing licenses for Ontario were discontinued. (Women were exempted in 1969.) The returns did not warrant the book-work involved.

Algonquin Park had its first and only commercial fishing project, because of meat shortage, during the latter years of World War I. Jack Whitton was a butcher by trade in the village of Whitney. Jack was given a contract to net whitefish and lake trout in Lake Opeongo, sixteen miles away. The journey took four hours each way. It was a slow and laborious trip since the horse and wagon used the old railway spur-line bed as the road.

There are no files on this project and therefore it is not known what size mesh was used in the nets but it would not have been worth Whitton's time to gut and pack a fish weighing less than two pounds. Whitton probably procured some fish weighing ten, fifteen and up to thirty pounds. (The largest fish ever caught in Lake Opeongo weighed fifty pounds.)

The late George Holmberg, a former ranger, worked as a youth in the blacksmith shop of the Booth Lumber Company. After accompanying Whitton on a trip he decided something had to be done to the road bed to make it less jarring. He shaped two immense iron hooks and fastened them to the back wheel-base of the wagon. As the horses plodded along, the hooks heaved up the old railroad ties. On later journeys Holmberg chained several of the ties together and this was dragged along until the road-bed was somewhat improved.[3]

Once the highway was completed the fisheries administration at Toronto became concerned about the anticipated increase on angling pressure in the Park. As a result the Fisheries Research Laboratory was established in 1936 at Lake Opeongo under the direction of Dr. W. J. K. Harkness. This laboratory was re-named the Harkness Laboratory of Fisheries Research in 1961 in memory of the late Dr. W. J. K. Harkness, Chief, Fish and Wildlife Branch, Department of Lands and Forests.

The first staff used the buildings of an abandoned construction camp at Costello Lake until there were enough permanent buildings erected to house the full staff at Sproule Bay, Lake Opeongo.

The early surveys of fish distribution and investigations on the physical, chemical and biological conditions of the lakes in the area pointed out the unproductive nature of the Algonquin waters.

For several years speckled and lake trout fry were planted in the lakes bordering the railroad. Particular mention was made in Mark Robinson's diaries in 1922, 1923 and 1924 of large plantings of fish in the Algonquin lakes.

Other experiments were carried out in an attempt to increase the fish population. A lake closure system, on an alternate year basis, was initiated in 1938 as an experiment in fisheries' management and conservation. Since lake trout are very vulnerable to winter angling, no ice fishing was allowed after 1955.

The life histories of lake and speckled trout are now quite well known, and present research is still concerned with a study of the reproduction with special reference to the survival of eggs and young.

There has been an intensive study on splake which were introduced to the Algonquin waters in 1954. Splake is a cross between brook trout and lake trout. The spawning tendencies are most interesting to watch. While a speckled trout spawns on gravel bottoms, the splake spawns on rubble in a fashion similar to lake trout.

Fisheries research. Recording data on fish caught in Lake Lavieille.

One of the first known plantings of adult smallmouth bass was in 1898 by A. W. Fleck, when he stocked one of the lakes on his Rock Lake property.[4]

G.W. Bartlett stocked Cache Lake with parent bass in 1899[5] because J.S. Willison, in the *Independent Journal*, December 9, 1908 wrote an article, part of which is as follows: *"One of the interesting routes in the Park is that of Cache Lake (headquarters), down the Madawaska River to Lake of Two Rivers. This latter body of water contains smallmouth bass of fabulous size and wondrous pugnacity.... A four pound bass takes the archer spinner and later forms the basis for the evening meal."*

This description gives the erroneous impression that the Algonquin waters provide the right environment for rapid

Ice fishing.

growth. Also bass reproduction is very limited. Lake Opeongo, a lake of twenty-three square miles, returns to anglers an average of only six hundred bass a year.

Splake.

Many other aspects of aquatic biology have been studied at this research laboratory. A list of the publications and reports resulting in whole or in part of the work can be obtained from the Ministry of Natural Resources.

In 1944, Professor W.J.K. Harkness offered the use of the laboratories at Opeongo to the Forest Protection Branch. They tested the possibility of eliminating forest pests, especially the spruce budworm which was attacking the spruce and balsam fir. The effects of the D.D.T. spray on the fish, insect and mammal life of the area were investigated. The dangers of using D.D.T. do not seem to have been recognized in these studies, since it was used throughout Ontario as a forest pesticide in subsequent years.

The preservation of wildlife was another of the main concerns of the founders of Algonquin Park. In the superintendent's first annual report, Peter Thomson states: *"Mink, otter, fisher and marten are plentiful; there are many bear and wolves; the bear do very little damage but the wolves are destructive; Prairie chickens should be introduced into the Park."*

Elk and caribou were introduced in 1897 but the project was a failure. The main food of the caribou is lichens and there are not enough growing in the Park to support this animal. There

Fish ladder at Joe Lake. The Lakes and Rivers Improvement Act of 1927 required that when old dams were replaced, a fishway be provided. The fishways were sometimes a nuisance as fisheries biologists often did not want fish moving from one lake to another. The fish ladder at the Ragged-Smoke Lake dam was plugged to prevent other species from migrating into the excellent Ragged Lake trout waters.

are no records of caribou living below the French River district.[6]

In the early thirties a second attempt to establish elk in Algonquin was made. Mark Robinson has a notation in his diary on April 5, 1934: "Cow elk found drowned in Cranberry (Canisbay) Lake. Animal was opened and it was found that the cow would have produced a male calf." A single elk buck was seen many times at Cache Lake during that same summer but eventually disappeared.

Another impractical venture was trying to introduce wild turkeys which could not survive because of the heavy depth of snow. Capercaille from Norway was also unsuccessful. George Bartlett kept exotic fowl in cages as an attraction for the tourists but the administration at Toronto rightly decided that keeping caged birds in a wilderness park was not a good policy.

In James Wilson's report, written after his exploratory trip through the Park, he was very emphatic in stating that "not only wolves but bears and foxes should be destroyed without mercy." Like Thomson, he suggested destroying loons and gulls because they were depleting the fish population. In 1894 man definitely did not consider the importance of the balance of nature! George Bartlett never swerved from his belief that all wolves should be destroyed. He repeatedly emphasized the importance of destroying as many wolves as possible. The Park Act provided for a special license issued by the Com-

Ranger Art Briggs with a poisoned wolf.

missioner of Crown Lands for the destruction of wolves, bear and other wild and noxious animals but the rangers' permits only mentioned wolves.

The use of poisoned bait to kill wolves was discontinued in the early 1920s because too many other valuable mammals and birds also died from eating the poisoned bait. However, the rangers continued to hunt wolves by using snares and guns, although it was seldom that the wily wolf could be killed by a bullet. Very often a wolf was able to chew the snare and free itself. One wolf that was finally snared had two other wires around its neck. Ed Godin, one of the rangers, was determined that he would experiment with different grades of wire until he found one that a wolf could not chew. He finally succeeded and in 1930 he killed twenty wolves within a six-month period.

Although wolves have been hunted for more than fifty years in Algonquin Park they continue to be heard and are seen occasionally. It has taken many dead wolves and extensive research to convince the public that the wolf has an important part to play in maintaining the balance of nature. Even the Park staff, who had previously believed that as many wolves as possible should be destroyed, eventually began to see their error. The wolf bounty was rescinded by Royal assent on December 15, 1972.

One eerie experience with wolves was told of by Mark Robinson. He was walking through Sims' Pit one September day when a dense fog closed in, blocking out all visibility. Robin-

Steve Waters found nine wolves dead and frozen near the poisoned bait he had put out on North Tea Lake. He stood some of them up to take this macabre group photo.

Author Lacey Amy with park staff, 1911. Left to right, Superintendent G. W. Bartlett, Amy, Jim Bartlett and Mark Robinson.

son stood quietly in one spot, waiting for the mist to clear away. Everything was silent. Soon Robinson became aware of barely discernible movements around him. As he watched he noticed that the shadowy forms seemed to be closing in. He decided they were wolves and that they were using this method to try and discover what the alien "something" was. Robinson fired two shots with his revolver and the wolves disappeared as quietly as they had appeared. (Whenever Robinson told of the experience he would come to the conclusion that it was a "once in a lifetime happening.")

Some of the old-time rangers enjoyed telling hair-raising yarns about animals, often with more exaggeration than truth if they thought the listeners were gullible. They stretched their stories for the benefit of Lacey Amy, a well known author of boys' adventure stories, who had come up to the Park to learn about wolves. Lacey Amy "turned the tables" on the rangers when he wrote *The Blue Wolf*. The wolf-plot in the story far surpassed anything a bushman could have possibly dreamed up!

Deer have always been one of the main attractions in the Park, especially when seen in a natural wilderness setting. Even before the highway was finished the deer had learned

Wolf capers, 1912. The older rangers enjoyed staging alarming scenes with wolf carcasses.

Steve Waters was stationed at Rock Lake on the border of the Park. Fall hunters would get off at the station and travel down to their hunting camps outside the Park boundaries. Steve made this decoy as a joke, to see how they would react.

that there would be "hand-outs" at the hotels and at other permanent homes.

The Algonquin Hotel had three deer that stayed near their stable all winter. "Beauty," a well-known deer, was around Joe Lake for three years and became quite a favourite. One stormy winter evening, Mark Robinson could hear wolves howling and yipping very close to his house. All at once he heared frantic stamping on the veranda and he opened the door to investigate. Beauty was pressed close to the wall and, out in front of the house, the wolves were keeping their distance but still howling. They slunk away as soon as they saw Robinson.

Beauty and her offspring, as well as the larger herd of tame deer at Cache Lake, kept the tourists entertained summer after summer by accepting food from their hands.

A buck deer and doe.

During the later World War I years there was a scarcity of meat. To alleviate the crisis the Ontario Government decided that, since deer were over-abundant in Algonquin Park, it would be a good move to harvest a couple of thousand animals. The deer population had reached such a high peak that there was really not sufficient food available to carry them through the winter. The project didn't get started until late in the fall of 1917 and only five hundred animals, totalling about sixty-two thousand pounds of meat, were shipped out of the Park.[7]

In the past few years, however, the highway deer that had attracted thousands of tourists to Algonquin have been diminishing. Several causes have been considered: the widening and straightening of the highway took away the quiet hideouts that the deer previously had; the increased rushing traffic whizzing by might have frightened them; there have been several consecutive winters of heavy snowfall; they were not able to reach their green foliage food supply because their "browse" had grown too high; there was no new browse growing because there had been practically no forest fires. Lumbering operations had not been extensive enough to produce large areas suitable for such growth and the deer population had begun to spread out into areas where their food supply was available. Wolves, their main predator, do not seem to be a contributing factor to the fewer numbers.[8]

Moose are more able to find sufficient food in winter. Their legs are longer and they are able to walk over a fairly tall sapling. Their heavy body holds the tree down while they feed on the green parts. It has been said that moose do not "yard up" in large numbers as the deer do. Occasionally a person may be fortunate to see a few huge depressions in the snow where moose, as they rested, melted and packed the snow.

Moose keep moving their resting places as they search for a better feeding area. Moose have a variety of ways to find food. One most unusual way was observed by Mark Robinson:

"One day I noticed moose tracks in the snow that were going only in one direction. I followed to investigate and came to a small spring-fed pond that wasn't entirely frozen over. A moose was standing in the water with only its back showing about eighteen inches above the surface. The moose brought its head up and I saw that it had a big mouthful of finely leafed pond plants dripping from its mouth."

Mark Robinson inspecting a "bear-claw tree." Naturalists used to think that bear marked their territory by reaching up to claw the bark as high as possible. Later research has not substantiated this.

Bears are another major tourist attraction. Their behaviour is so unpredictable that Park visitors have to be warned continually to observe them only at a distance.

Bears became accustomed to people when the lumber camps operated in the Park. They began visiting the garbage dumps and then, becoming bolder, they started raiding the storehouses. Cooks, collectively, seem to have been more terrified of bears than any other bushworkers.

On more than one occasion Mark Robinson was summoned to go over to a nearby camp cook-house to dispose of a bear. One of the occasions would have been hilarious if the cook hadn't been so frightened. There he was, perched up on one of the rafters, brandishing a long butcher knife and screaming incoherently in French. Bruin didn't pay the slightest attention to the commotion and kept on hauling down slabs of bacon hanging from the same rafter.

Before the present huge incinerator was installed at Algonquin Park, each hotel and camp had its own garbage dump and most of the cottages each had a small one. Canoe-trippers were very careless and left food behind them also. This added up to an endless supply of food for the bear and a vast accumulation of litter.

1953 was a peak bear population year—too many bears and too little food with a poor berry crop doing its part to make the situation critical. The hungry bears smashed their way into cottages and left havoc and destruction behind them. George Heintzman, a ranger at Lake Opeongo, snared four bear near his shelter hut and was forced to shoot three more.

Drastic measures had to be taken. Campers were given garbage bags before they started on canoe trips and they were asked to bring the bags out filled with garbage and to deposit them in movable bins that were enclosed within heavily wired fencing. The bins were emptied into the incinerator daily. If the public continues to cooperate, the worry about "garbage" bears will be, it is hoped, a thing of the past.

Very limited wildlife research had been carried on before 1920. Dr. Allan Cleghorn did a detailed study on *The Occurrence of Rabies in Animals* and his paper was published in 1912. At the same time Dr. Cleghorn was making a study on the hibernation of mammals.

In 1944, a thirty-square-mile area was set aside as a natural undisturbed environment for students and biologists to research and produce information on the relationship of wildlife to their environment. The main laboratory is located on Lake Sasajewan, one mile north of Highway 60, opposite the Mew Lake campsite.

It has been essential to restrict public travel in this research area because man can and does disturb the delicate balance of nature.

One of the main species of wildlife studies in the Park has been the beaver. Beaver are important to the economy of the country, especially in forested areas. They also have a pronounced effect on other forest animals and their environment through the damming of streams and flooding new territory.

Beaver populations fluctuate but they do not seem to follow a regular cycle as do grouse, hares and mice. When beaver numbers are high, as they are right now in Ontario, it is difficult to deplete their numbers in Algonquin since trapping is not allowed in most of the area.

Live-trapping of beaver has been done in Algonquin many times. G. W. Bartlett sent many animals to zoos in other parts of the world until it became too expensive. In the early 1940s several animals were live-trapped and sent to the Moosonee area of James Bay where disease and over-trapping had almost eradicated the beaver. For the same reasons beaver were transported to both the Rupert House district and to the Patricia district in northern Ontario during the 1950s. The beaver that were sent to Europe and Asia have adapted to their new locations very well.

Beaver are another one of the main tourist attractions in

This photograph of rangers Bartlett and Robinson shows strikingly how the beaver changed the water level, flooding surrounding forest and killing the trees.

the Park. People have been known to spend hours quietly waiting beside a pond for a glimpse of a beaver. These animals have an acute sense of hearing and smell and, although their eye-sight is poor, it isn't often that they are caught by predators. At the first awareness of danger, beaver swimming through the surface of the water will slap their tails as a warning, then dive and swim under water. They will

A nineteen-day-old beaver. Note the dextrous front feet. The curved toe-nails help the animal to dig tunnels. The webbed hind feet bear a pincer-like nail on the second toe, which is used in grooming.

Otters depend upon the beaver to provide a suitable habitat and will sometimes take over an abandoned beaver lodge.

surface, smell and listen for signs of danger and, if all is safe, will continue with their activities.

There has been research on other animals at the Wildlife Station: investigations on marten and fisher, which are common in the Park but not elsewhere in the Province, have been carried on; deer and wolves and their relationship to each other have been studied for years with the hope of producing a more intelligent approach to their management; studies of parasites and diseases affecting wild animals is another very important phase of the research.

Biting insects (mosquitoes, black flies and no-seeums) are a bother to both people and animals, especially in the spring and early summer. Loggers, construction workers and other people involved in outdoor activities are sometimes greatly hampered by these nuisances.

Most forest animals are not bothered as badly from insects' bites as humans seem to be, even though they are known to transmit diseases from one animal to another.

Newcomers to the woods talk by the hour about the miseries they suffer. Early exploration reports often made mention of these pests. Champlain, in 1604, described "hosts of mosquitoes so thick that they hardly allowed us to draw breath, so greatly and severely did they persecute us."[9] (He did not differentiate between black flies and mosquitoes.) An 1869 astronomical report mentions, "I really think that they work their stings like a needle of a sewing machine.... They attacked me with an impetuosity truly marvellous, where one fell two took its place."

The Indians learned to live with the black fly and mosquito and probably developed a certain immunity to their bites. For people who intend to be in the bush a great deal, either for work or pleasure, it might help to accept the presence of biting insects and attempt to ignore them.

Early explorers, geologists and surveyors were interested in natural science and James Dickson, who surveyed throughout this part of Ontario, kept notes on what he observed. In *Camping in the Muskoka Region* he says:

"A loon suddenly plunges screaming into the water, and, propelled by both foot and wing, dashes out into the open lake.... The loon, having no joint in the leg, cannot walk, and is never found on shore far from water. We run in behind a sheltering ledge of rock, and step on shore. There on the bare ground, a few feet from the water, is a little black ball of down... a small black bill and pair of sharp eyes are visible.... The little fellow is evidently only a few hours out of the broken shell, which is lying to one side."

James Dickson was not only alerted to movements on the water but on the land too. He says:

Loons, with their haunting cries, are characteristic of the Park. Like many water-birds, the loon may flap its wings and run across the water to divert an intruder from the young.

"But what pattering is that we have heard on the hill-side, as if some animal were taking a single heavy step at a time.... We pause beneath a tall green pine and listen.... Next we feel a smart slap on one shoulder, when, looking up, one of the green cones which grow near the top of the pine just misses our face.... We look up. The mystery is at once explained. High up... where the cones are most numerous, a tiny squirrel is seen running from limb to limb, and with his sharp teeth nipping off cone after cone; and if we choose to remain long enough, we will see the little gentleman run head-first down the tree, seize one of the newly-plucked cones, seat himself on a log, and, holding it between his forepaws, tear off the green husks with his teeth, and make his breakfast of the soft white pith within."

Steve Waters, one of the first rangers, was a keen observer. Notes from his diaries mention trailing arbutus blooming and an April 12 arrival date of the winter wren—"plucky little thing." During one of the winters he kept some meat hanging outside for the birds to feed on. His feathered visitors were Arctic three-toed woodpeckers, downy woodpeckers, bluejays, pine grosbeaks, chickadees and nuthatches. Waters says he was never lonely, because there was so much happening. On one occasion he noticed a peculiar movement a half mile out on the ice at Lake Opeongo. The ice looked as if it were heaving and bulging in an uneven line. At one spot a black head appeared and Steve recognized it as that of an otter which had broken through the three-quarter inch thick ice.[10]

Each changing season brought its own special brand of magic. R. P. Little tells us:

"Spring is sweet in the northland for it is so long delayed.... Where was spring? Spring began in March when the snow lay deepest; spring was there in April when the creeks were high and the ice melted around the shore of the lake while the snow was still deep and the snowshoe rabbits ran on the crust where the wolves could not follow; and spring was there in

May when the ice was black and the snow was melted in spots and you saw a loon fly out of the south with wild cries and pass overhead while winter melted into spring and summer burst in overnight with a great wind and rain."

Little goes on to say:

"Take the autumn: there is a silence about it, a stillness, a sense of something impending, like the breathless pause before the bursting of a storm. The red and yellow hills are slowly deepening in colour and the soft wind blows all day and drifts the leaves as silently as feathers. There is a dead-leaf perfume in the air and the sweet smell of Indian grass."[11]

In the early years the rangers did not get any weather reports. Instead they became quite proficient at predicting the weather from watching cloud formations, listening to the wind and observing the behaviour of the birds and animals. Mark Robinson heard the shrill call of the "cock of the woods" (pileated woodpecker) as it flew from a pine "shako" one day. He quickly turned and looked carefully at the sky. There was no sign of a storm, but he heeded the warning and cut his patrol short. A couple of hours after he got back to the shelter house, the storm had broken.

Mark Robinson kept two well-filled feeding trays at the Joe Lake shelter house. The birds arrived and fed by day and the mice, flying squirrels and an ermine came in the evenings. The wood mice scampered up the stand and fed on the tray itself; the flying squirrels glided down from the roof and trees to the tray and ate the food while the ermine crouched below waiting impatiently for an evening meal of either mouse or squirrel.

The flying squirrels seemed to take great delight in teasing the ermine. They would peek over the edge of the tray, then flip up onto its roof, jump to a tree or the roof of the house, then saucily glide down fairly close to the ermine before quickly running up another tree. At the same time the ermine would be crouched, ready to spring at his victim and, seeing it disappear, would snarl and bare his vicious teeth. With a final snarl, and flashing his bright red tongue, he would lunge off into the forest. This became a nightly performance and each time Robinson heard the pattering on his roof he knew that the flying squirrel had won the battle of wits once again.

The youth camps included natural science in their daily programs. Possibly the Taylor Statten Camps on Canoe Lake, by inviting well-known naturalists as interim staff, had the most enthusiastic program. Jack Miner, Stuart Thompson, Ernest Thompson Seton, as well as Mark Robinson who was always on call, were a few who visited the camp.

Thompson Seton came to Camp Ahmek primarily to get an

Left to right, Mark Robinson, Ernest Thompson Seton, Stuart Thompson, Taylor Statten at Canoe Lake Station, 1922.

Indian Lore program started. Seton was a real showman with lots of contagious enthusiasm and it wasn't long before a council-ring was constructed. Each evening an impressive Indian pow-wow was held in the ring. There was time set aside for the campers, if they had observed anything unusual in the woods that day, to mention what they had seen. Any councillors who had passed rigid tests to become "braves" were presented with buckskin Indian costumes and were accepted into the "tribe" at an impressive Indian ceremony.[12]

No matter where Seton travelled he asked innumerable questions and kept copious notes about the animals and the

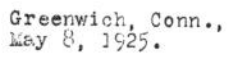

Greenwich, Conn.,
May 8, 1925.

Ranger Mark Robinson,
Algonquin Park,
Ontario, Canada.

My dear Ranger:

Have you time to tell me something about the Wolverine? Are there any in the Park? Did you ever hear of any in Ontario, south of the Park? How about Marten this year? & Fisher

With kind regards,

Yours cordially,

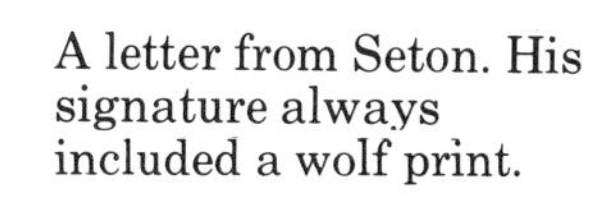

A letter from Seton. His signature always included a wolf print.

A deer mouse is readily tamed.

forests of each new place he visited. He kept up a lively correspondence with Mark Robinson over the years.

The first Canadian nature trail was cut out through the forest behind Camp Ahmek. The resident naturalist, Colin Farmer, planned the trail so it would wind through swamps as well as hardwood and coniferous woods and had the campers help label points of interest. Once it was completed Jack Miner cut the ribbon and officially opened the trail in 1926. Many parents who came to visit their children at camp were pleased to be able to walk the trail by themselves and learn from the labels the names of different plants and trees.[13]

Professor J. R. Dymond, a biologist as well as a naturalist, had a cottage on Smoke Lake. In 1942 he introduced an occasional nature walk to interest the cottagers in the world about them. They were so successful that other tourists, hearing about them, asked if they could join the group.

Two years later F. A. MacDougall, Deputy Minister of Lands and Forests, asked "J.R.," as he was known, to plan a nature program for all Park visitors, emphasizing the importance of the Park as a sanctuary. Some of the suggested topics to be covered were rock and soil formations, erosion, fire protection, plant succession, game fish and the interdependence of plants and animals.

By 1944 three nature trails had been cut and some of the more common plants, shrubs and trees were labelled. A temporary nature centre, under the direction of Al Helmsley, was set up in tents at the parking lot at the beginning of the Canisbay Trail. Conducted nature hikes and a weekly evening program at the Cache Lake recreation centre were scheduled.

The program was so enthusiastically received that it was necessary to start making plans for a permanent visitors' centre. The present one, at Found Lake at mileage 13, was opened in 1953. Visitors, by viewing exhibits and displays, get an introduction to Algonquin's forest, fish, flora, wildlife and history. The more serious tourists can study the various collections of plants, birds and mammals more thoroughly on request. The building is open daily, with a Park Naturalist on duty, throughout the summer season from late June to after the September Labour Day holiday. It is also open on weekends from Victoria Day to after Thanksgiving.

The "museum" has been enlarged and now includes a theatre where movies are shown each day, starting on the hour.

The interpretive program, as it has done in the past, is continuing to help people to appreciate their natural environment. It stresses the importance of preserving it for the future. This is very necessary: for instance, the upsurge of interest in eating wild edible plants. In *Algonquin Park Archaeology, 1971* there is a summary article by Love (1966) listing a number of edible plants found in Algonquin Park. The article was orientated toward lost campers striving for a few days' subsistence and not toward a band of ten to fifteen people camping for many days. The saying, "Just look, leave them for others to see" is a rule in all Provincial Parks. If everyone will adhere to this ruling, endangered species will not disappear.

A glance over the years at the interpretive program clearly shows how successful it has been: there is one twenty-mile hiking trail; several nature trails of varying lengths; and three other trails, each stressing a special aspect—the Lookout Trail features the geology of the area, the Hardwood Trail emphasizes forest ecology, and the Beaver Pond Trail shows how beaver have changed the environment.

The Algonquin interpretive staff first organized public wolf howls in August 1970. It is undoubtedly the highlight of all the programs offered—they are a "howling" success, wolves or no answering wolves.

At one of the "howls" twenty-four hundred people in six hundred cars drove down the highway—much too large and cumbersome. A maximum of two hundred and fifty cars is allowed in the theatre parking lot for the preliminary part of the program.[14] It is quite amazing that such a large number of people can be quiet enough to hear an answering howl. Even if the wolves do not answer, there are many other night sounds that are exciting—the gnawing sound of a wood beetle, a cricket chirping, a distant eerie call of a loon, or the echo from the warning slap of a beaver's tail on the water.

A research student howling in an attempt to receive an answer from wolves.

What good is this varied program? It provides interest; it opens up a whole new horizon for the curious; public education is necessary for public cooperation in such spheres as fish and game regulations, forest fire prevention; and it gives the public an opportunity to learn more about the resource projects that are being studied.

The Pioneer Logging Exhibit, located just inside the East Gate, was opened in 1959. The path from the parking lot to the main exhibit has show-cases displaying photographs and sketches of early logging operations. There is a full scale model of a camboose shanty, a saddle-back locomotive and a huge white pine log representative of the size that was cut during the late 1800s.

Algonquin Park has produced and still is printing valuable information folders. The 1967 *General Information and Canoe Route* folder, illustrated with six Tom Thomson paintings, is spectacular and is still available. Check lists are available at the museum as well as booklets giving information about four of the walking trails.

The Raven, a weekly bulletin, has been printed since 1963 and is available free to the public. It gives information as to

Now on display at the Pioneer Logging Exhibit, this saddle-back locomotive was used at the Booth and Shannon sawmills, Biscotasing.

the times and places for scheduled nature hikes and the topics for the different evening programs. Mr. R. J. Rutter has been the editor for several years. He has written many instructive articles on natural science and history of the Park. On request, thousands of the season's complete set of bulletins are mailed out each fall.

Algonquin Artists

"Algonquin Park was chiefly enjoyed by American visitors and a few eccentric artists and nature lovers" before World War I. So claims *Renewing Nature's Wealth.*

In fact, there were many Canadians visiting the Park between 1905 and 1914.

In 1902, artists belonging to the Toronto Art Students' League came to Algonquin Park to sketch. Robert Holmes, W.W. Alexander and David Thompson had heard enthusiastic reports of a canoe trip that had been taken by the son of the Honourable G.W. Ross the previous summer, with Tim O'Leary as a ranger-guide. They decided that it was the place to go and they wrote O'Leary, asking if he would take them on a similar trip. O'Leary met the three artists at Canoe Lake Station and they were off on their canoe/sketching trip.

Their motto, *Nulla Dies Sine Linea*—"no day without a line"—slowed down their travel time so much that O'Leary

An Algonquin scene by W. W. Alexander, 1903.

Pipe Corpse Plant by Robert Holmes, 1903.

was beginning to wonder if the party would ever reach their destination on schedule. Robert Holmes always wanted to finish a water-colour of a particular plant in its natural setting; Thompson, who was fascinated by beaver dams and houses, also wanted to get all the details into his sketch before moving on; and Alexander's specialty of sketching fast moving water needed to be completed on location, too. On the very few times that the artists grumbled about a rather mediocre campsite, O'Leary would say, "Wait, boys, until I get you to Lake Opeongo and the Sunnyside cabin—it is a veritable King Edward Hotel."[1]

When the artists returned to Toronto, their fervour knew no bounds. Their descriptions of the superlative Algonquin scenery inspired other artists to go until it became the accustomed thing for artists to plan a sketching trip to Algonquin Park. It was Tom McLean's glowing accounts that led Tom Thomson to take his first trip in May 1912 with fellow-artist, H. B. Jackson (no relation of "A. Y."). Jackson says this trip was more of a fishing trip to Tom than a sketching trip. But Tom did do "a few notes, sky-lines and colour effects."

Sunnyside cabin on Lake Opeongo.

The Canoe by Tom Thomson, 1914.

Thomson had had practically no experience in paddling a canoe, since the Thomson family had always used a row-boat on Georgian Bay. The two artists loaded their canoe at the Mowat dock in the "teeth of a southerly gale." Shannon Fraser was watching them pack their canoe and suspected that they did not know too much about canoeing. He suggested that they stay with him over night and start off on their trip in the morning. Before they went into the house, Thomson supposedly said to Fraser, "Don't let the fellow I am with know that I am not a good canoeman or he won't go with me."

Thomson was known to never do anything by halves once he became interested in a project and this certainly must have been true with his canoeing. For once Jackson had returned to Toronto, Thomson was expert enough to travel alone by canoe.

Jackson tells us that people often misunderstood Thomson, thinking that he wasn't interested in people. This was not true, but if he became absorbed in whatever he was doing he was absolutely oblivious to what was happening around him, a tendency he may have inherited from his father.

(There is a delightful true story about John Thomson taking his wife, driving by horse and buggy, to Owen Sound to shop. Mrs. Thomson went shopping and Mr. Thomson went to the library. Thomson was able to get a book he had particularly wanted to read. Greatly pleased, he hurried back home and began to read his new book. Some time later, one of the girls asked their father where mother was. Thomson, looking surprised, said, "Did I take her to town?" Two of the girls, instead of father, hitched up the horse and went back to town to pick up mother.)[2]

It is debatable as to whether Thomson was able to get a guide's license that first summer, but he may have, since his uncanny ability to catch fish and his reputation as an expert campfire cook soon became well-known. In any case, whether he was a friend or a guide with Leonard Mack and Harry Bracken in July 1912, Leonard Mack wrote Thomson in March 1913: "But I still have a very lively recollection of the trip and both Harry and myself feel very grateful to you for all that you did (and it was considerable) to add to the pleasures of the trip." A tribute to a true woodsman!

Sketch for *West Wind* by Tom Thomson. It was offered to Mark Robinson in the fall of 1915. Robinson thought it was so good that Thomson should keep it and make a canvas of it.

Thomson guided in 1913, sometimes as a second guide with George Rowe but often on his own. Even with more jobs available than guides to fill them, it was hard to break into the "first choice circle." The regular guides took every opportunity to down-play the newer guides. At an Algonquin Park hotel regatta in 1915 two guides were overheard discussing Thomson in a disparaging way. A third person spoke up and said, "If either of you could paddle a canoe as well as Thomson can fish and paint, you would be rated the top guides in Ontario."

Thomson did some emergency fire-fighting during 1913 and even considered applying for a permanent Park staff position. In a letter he writes,

"I thought of putting in my application for a park Ranger's job and went down to Headquarters with that idea but there is so much red tape about it that I might not get on for months so I will try and get work in some Engraving shop for a few months this winter."

It was in 1914 that the phrase "The Canadian Algonquin School of Art" came into being. Thomson, by this time, had a thorough knowledge of the north and was literally part of it. His ability to transport himself entirely into the wilderness was very evident. He wanted to have his fellow artists come to Algonquin to share this inspiration. They arrived at Mowat in late September until the "woods were full of painters."

Thomson found the next year rather slow at Algonquin. Because of the war there weren't as many tourists needing guides and many of his friends were in the army and couldn't come to the Park. Thomson did some fire-fighting and stayed around Mowat until July 10 which was later than usual. He also seems to have done a fair amount of vagabond wandering. Tom was patriotic and it worried him that, for physical reasons, he could not be taking part in the war effort.

The Blecher family of Buffalo, who had owned one of the Gilmour mill houses since 1905, inadvertently did their small part to build up patriotic fervour—Mrs. Blecher was determined she was going to fly their American flag by itself.

Mark Robinson had informed the family, through the son, Martin, that they could fly the American flag in Canada only if the Union Jack or the Canadian ensign flew above it. The guests at Mowat Lodge began to get interested in what would happen if the Blechers did not give in to this ultimatum. No change by the Blecher family was made but, mysteriously, on two consecutive nights the rope was cut, but each of the following mornings, the American flag was up again.

On the third morning, some of the Mowat guests noticed Thomson sitting on the veranda with field glasses. Every

The sign painted in oils by Tom Thomson.

once in a while, he would focus them on the Blecher property. Looking up at the flagpole, the guests noticed a very tiny Union Jack flying above the large Stars and Stripes. Unknown to anyone, Thomson had bought the small Union Jack and had put it up during the night. With a quiet smile, he was waiting to see what would develop.

Mark Robinson decided he had better go down and speak to Mrs. Blecher and to suggest, again, that the Union Jack must fly over the American flag. Mrs. Blecher, by this time, was quite irate about being forced to do something she didn't want to do. She proceeded to chase Robinson off their property, wildly swinging a broom as she ran. Robinson, as well as the tourists, had quite a laugh over the episode. (The Blechers finally complied with the ruling.)

During the summer of 1916 Thomson fire-ranged for the full season with Ned Godin, as his ranger-partner. They were stationed at Achray, on Grand Lake, not far from the Ontario Forestry Branch headquarters. Thomson found that he had very little time for sketching. He did find time to paint a sign for the cabin—"Out-Side-In"— that remained there for years. Professor T. W. Dwight had been promised the sign if it were ever taken down. He did not receive it, nor does he know what eventually happened to it.

Thomson made a weekly trip by canoe and tote road to Basin Depot for supplies and mail. William Hughes, the Park ranger for this "berth," often took him home for a meal. Mrs.

William Jim Hughes, who became a ranger in 1912, enjoyed wearing this buckskin outfit made by his mother-in-law.

Lawren Harris and Dr. James MacCallum went with Thomson to the Petawawa section of the Park in fall 1916. They were so busy painting and fishing there was no time to bother with shaving. Lawren Harris took this picture of Thomson the day before they returned to civilization.

Moving day for the Hughes family and the Brent Lumber Company, 1916.

Hughes and her younger sister still talk about the good times they had together. Usually the time was spent by Mrs. Hughes crocheting and the other three playing cards. Thomson was fascinated with the intricate designs that Mrs. Hughes produced. One evening when he was delayed by a storm Tom took out his pen and drew a pattern for her.[3]

The Hughes were moved to Brent, on Cedar Lake, that fall and did not see Thomson again. It wasn't until after his death that the Hughes learned that Tom was an artist. Thomson had, as usual, never spoken about himself or his work. The Hughes only knew that he was "handy with his pen."

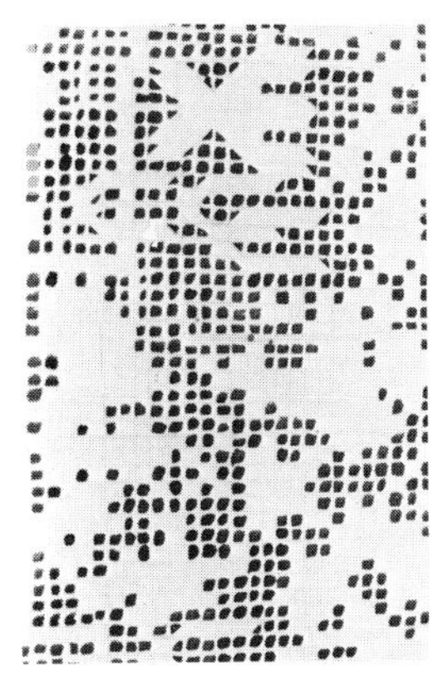

Tom Thomson's crochet pattern for Mrs. Hughes. Because he knew little about crochet-work, the pattern is next to impossible to follow.

On July 8, 1917, Tom Thomson was drowned in Canoe Lake. Thomson's friends planned to build a commemorative cairn on the hill above his campsite. Bill Beatty, an artist but not a Group of Seven member, did a great deal of the heavy work in hauling the stones up the hillside. J. E. MacDonald composed the wording and designed the inscription. MacDonald was a member of the Group of Seven, and Thomson had visited his home frequently.

Very few of Thomson's artist-friends ever returned to Algonquin to paint after his death. A. Y. Jackson, writing from overseas, probably expressed their mutual thoughts when he said, "Without Tom the north country seems a desolation of bush and rock. He was the guide, the interpreter...."

Taylor Statten had had a life-long interest in the arts and he planned his camp's programs to stimulate this same interest in the councillors and campers. Tom Thomson had become a legendary figure to the "Canoe-Lakers" and it wasn't difficult to keep everyone enthusiastic. There were many sketching trips to the cairn and each camper produced a quota of "art" which was saved for the big show in August.

Someone suggested having a totem pole carved, depicting Thomson's achievements and death. Jack Ridpath, an expert wood-carver, carved the totem and the painting was done by the councillors.

Taylor Statten made elaborate and careful plans for the

Summer Night by Thoreau MacDonald. Son of Group of Seven painter J. E. H. MacDonald, Thoreau MacDonald is a well known designer and illustrator, with a love of outdoor scenes. This scene of Thomson fishing was one of a series of twelve illustrations for *Canadian Forum* magazine in 1927.

Thomson day, August 16th, 1930, when the totem pole would be unveiled. The National Gallery loaned the camp twenty-five original Thomson sketches, which were carefully guarded and hung in a separate building. All the campers' "masterpieces" that had been painted over the summer, as well as some reproductions of Thomson canvasses, were hung in the big dining-room.

An impressive pageant was presented, just as the sun was setting. A flotilla of canoes and boats, full of people, floated on the water below the cairn and totem pole as Mark Robinson gave a brief talk before the unveiling. A birch bark canoe, filled with wild flowers, paddled by Bill Stoqua, the Indian canoe instructor at camp, drew up to the dock below. The flower-laden canoe was carried up the hill and placed at the base of the cairn.[4]

Bill Beatty continued to go up to the Park for several years. He often brought his students with him for outdoor sketching lessons. Robinson's January 1924 diary says, "Bill Beatty and Tom Stone are painting the bluffs down at the Cache Lake bridge." A. J. Casson, a later member of the "Group of Seven," still goes up to Algonquin to sketch.

Today the Park continues to be popular with wildlife artists and photographers. Robert Bateman painted a sketch of a gull flying at Sproule Bay, Lake Opeongo, when he was a student researcher at the Harkness Fisheries Laboratory in 1951.

The Tom Thomson totem pole.

Opeongo Gull by Robert Bateman, 1951.

Robinson Recollections

Perhaps the reader has noticed the heavy reliance placed on Mark Robinson's diaries, stories and experiences. He was my father. He was also one of the few rangers who was a naturalist and he enjoyed teaching others to be equally interested in everything they saw in the woods. Father had kept a diary that was more than a work-time-sheet and his set of Algonquin diaries is the only one in existence.

While it had originally been planned that there would be year-around accommodation for Park rangers' wives and families somewhere nearby, this plan had been made by someone who had not lived in the area. G. W. Bartlett, Superintendent of the Park, was himself a family man. He had learned from personal experience that even on the railroad line at Park Headquarters, problems arose because of the lack of schools and medical service, not to mention the isolation from friends and neighbours. Such a plan would be completely impractical. Bartlett tried to compensate for this by giving the rangers three holidays during the year at times when poaching wasn't rampant.

My twin sister, Elsie, and I were born after Dad went to the Park. He intended to be home for the event but we not only upset this well-laid plan by arriving early but decided to be two instead of one. Dad arrived back from a patrol trip to see several flags flying at Cache Lake (Bartlett's idea that something special should be done to celebrate the good news).

Since the Canoe Lake "berth" was too far away from the railroad for the rangers to keep adequately in touch with all the people coming in and departing on the trains, it was decided that a chief ranger's headquarters should be built at Joe Lake. It was to be large enough to accommodate extra staff—it had two bedrooms, a big main room, a summer kitchen and a veranda across the front. Underneath the main part there was an enclosed storage space for canoes and fire-fighting equipment. There was even a small insulated cool room for storing perishable food. This was reached through a trap-door in the kitchen floor. Instead of the usual log-type shelter, it was made of clapboard and painted white at a cost of one hundred and fifty dollars. The rangers moved their

The new Joe Lake shelter house, 1912.

belongings from the Canoe Lake "berth" to the Joe Lake station on October 5 while they worked at the new building. The big stone fire-place in the station provided adequate heat during the evenings until they moved into the shelter house on October 25, 1911.

Dad and his ranger-partners, first Jim Bartlett and then Bob Balfour, made additional improvements: a tool and wood shed was built; a stone wall was constructed; and below the wall, wheelbarrow after wheelbarrow of soil plus manure from the Algonquin Hotel stable were carted in readiness for a future vegetable garden. To make a safer play area for his small children on their holiday visits, our father hauled countless more loads of soil to fill in between the jutting rocks in front of the house. When two platforms had been constructed for tents, there was comfortable summer housing for all six Robinsons and for the ranger-partner as well.

Even after Dad had been given permission in 1912 to have his family at Joe Lake for July and August there were many difficulties that seemed insurmountable but our intrepid mother decided to "cross each bridge as she came to it." There were clothes for both warm and cool weather and extra bedding to be packed, as well as a crate of eggs, a crock of butter and countless other things.

We children started counting the hours before departure time a week ahead and were sure the great day would never arrive. It did. Trunks and boxes were transported to the Barrie station. The family was on its way. Even desolate Scotia Junction was a special place because it was there that passengers changed trains to reach Algonquin Park. Big sister read stories aloud during the two-hour wait. At last we climbed aboard and on this train the conductor and trainman knew who we were and did their best to help entertain us.

Two things of note always happened on this last lap of the journey that we never forgot: the train slowed down to a mere crawl as it inched its way slowly over the very high Cashman Creek trestle. This was done to keep the trestle structure from vibrating too much. The train slowed down again about three miles west of Brule Lake to give the passengers an opportunity to read:

ALGONQUIN NATIONAL PARK
SUMMIT GRADE AT RAIL LEVEL
1607 FEET

This sign was placed at the highest elevation along the Grand Trunk Railway in the Park.

As soon as we got off the train, there was so much to see: the beautiful log station that had only been built four years before, and the Algonquin Hotel on the hill, and the outfitting store, and the many canoes nearby on the shore and, across the bay, the comfortable white and green cottage that was the shelter house. Then the train engine began to puff, the whistle blew, and the train pulled out across the gravel fill and bridge and disappeared through a rock cut.

It isn't hard to imagine how many questions we four children were asking as the family walked along the railroad track: was the pet deer, Jenny, still around the cabin; was the mother bear still tearing up rotten logs, looking for a meal of ants; would we see the beaver working in the nearby marsh or hear the wolves howling? Dad's answer to each question was, "Wait and see but keep your eyes and ears open."

Mark Robinson and family canoeing.

Baked beans, lumberjack style, and Dad's home-made bread were a "must" for the first meal. It was rather a shock to discover there was only canned milk to drink, but after a few days the family didn't bother to comment on the difference.

The first task, after dinner, was to help take down the Union Jack. This, and raising the flag in the morning, was a daily task that was given to brother Jack to supervise.

The first big project was to learn to swim. No one was allowed to paddle a canoe alone until he could swim five hundred yards, upset the canoe in deep water, empty it, climb in again and paddle it back. Since the water was deep off the floating dock Dad devised a unique way to teach us to swim. A towel was tied around a child's tummy and three feet of rope, one end tied to the towel and the other to a long pike pole, was used to ease the child into the water. Partially supported by father holding the pole, one learned first to float and then "dog-paddle" until confidence was gained. Later, we were taught different swimming strokes.

On short canoe trips, only Dad paddled. He rarely travelled up the middle of a lake, preferring to skirt the shore-lines where everyone could see the different shore plants and shrubs. There was great excitement the day a phoebe's nest was spotted under an over-hanging cliff and still more when suddenly an otter, wakened from a sleep on a sunny rock, dived gracefully into the water.

Berry picking was the biggest summer undertaking. There were plenty of berry patches, the aftermath of lumbering or a regrowth area after forest fires. If given a choice of location, we always chose a place that was accessible only by canoe. Thus work and pleasure were combined. Also, since the lumbering was done along the shores in earlier years it meant that a patch could be chosen where the picker could work as well as watch what was happening on the water. For some reason the raspberries always grew larger in a brush heap and that meant that a person had to clamber over logs to get near enough to reach the huge berries. Too often one would go down, down and down to what seemed a bottomless pit, spilling berries at the same time. Amazingly, unless a hornet's nest had been disturbed, it was rather fun to try and extricate oneself.

Blueberrying was better but a person had to be sure-footed when walking on the steep rocks overhanging the water. The blueberries always looked larger and more luscious in the difficult spots. After a forest fire the biggest berries grew where the bushes crowded around a burned stump.

A rocky point was the favourite lunching spot. There was always a breeze and in a protected nook the water-striders darted here and there and sometimes a sizeable fish could be

Lunch after berry-picking.

seen lurking down in the cool shady water. Occasionally a porcupine would waddle past, apparently unaware of people (their eyesight is poor). And always there was bird song—the high musical notes of the white-throated sparrow, the bell-like call of the wood thrush, or the laughing call of the loon.

Later when everyone could swim well, we went berry-picking without the parents. First, the amount of berries to be picked was decided and then the berries were speedily gathered and set aside. Swimming and lunch came next and then a tramp over the hill to find out if there might be an unnamed lake which hadn't been mapped. Real adventure!

For the first few summers there were very few other children with whom to play but there was no difficulty in finding interesting activities to fill in the time. There was a big lumberman's flat-bottomed punt which was considered safe even for non-swimmers and it was in constant use. Big brother Jack, who was two years older than we twins, sometimes grumbled when he was asked to tumble out of bed at six o'clock to help paddle the heavy boat. He was the boat-builder of the family and supervised the construction of miniature sail boats. The faded cloth of discarded Algonquin National Park signs was used for the sails. When a race was organized, it was always his sail boat that won.

Each summer still another attempt was made to capture enough bullfrogs to have a frogs' leg dinner. Conservationist father told us we had to have at least six frogs to make a worthwhile meal. The required number was never attained.

The frogs were set free, but we had had the fun of catching them.

We had heard that the Scott family, who had leased a campsite on Buck (Tepee) creek for several years, once fed a pet bullfrog cooked macaroni. With this in mind, we kept one of the largest bullfrogs. He had a tremendous voice and he vented his frustration all night long at being moved. It kept the parents awake and next morning the order was given to recapture "that nuisance" and take it back up the lake to its own lily patch. Whereupon we learned that even a frog has to be in its own territory to be content.

There was a large wasps' nest in a spruce tree right beside the path leading to the wharf and yet no one was ever stung by them. They kept the flies away from the screen doors and away from anyone sitting on the veranda. A wasp would fly in, perch on the railing to watch and wait. The moment a fly landed on a person the wasp darted in, snipped it up and dashed off with its prey and another wasp would arrive to do similar sentinel duty.

Another time one of the twins crossed the railroad track to get a cool drink at the spring. (Family history claims that I was the twin involved, but I have no recollection of the incident.) She was only about two hundred yards from the cabin when a large timber wolf pulled himself up from the opposite side of a nearby shrub, glanced indifferently at her, and walked away. After a moment of watching the wolf she turned and came back to the cabin to tell the family. Dad laughed and said, "You probably disturbed the wolf's sleep and he was disgusted. The thing to remember is that he did not hurt you."

There was always a race between the Robinson children and the chipmunks as to who would get the most hazel nuts—the animals nearly always won. It wasn't exactly a

Brother Jack tells a fishing story to a visitor beside one of the Joe Lake family tents.

pleasureful job picking the prickly covered nuts but it was a challenge. One year there were great quantities. Father suggested that the nuts be spread on papers under a bed to dry. Just imagine our horror when one day, after returning from an all-day trip, we noticed the chipmunks had chewed a hole in the corner of the screen door and one emerged with his cheeks bulging with nuts. On investigation we discovered to our relief that only a few of the drying nuts had been transferred via the new opening.

It was a great honour to be chosen to be bow-man in the canoe. It wasn't easy to keep a watchful eye out for submerged stumps and dead-heads, especially if the sun was shining on a slightly rippled surface. Father's favourite admonition was "skin your eyes" and, unbelievable as it may sound, one could almost feel the peeling process taking place. One of our guests wrote a rhyme about father's sayings:

A ranger of fair Algonquin was he,
And his expressions were one, two, three.
The first he would say with a smirk
"Be careful or your eyes I'll scrape off with a chip."
And then, with a look at which kings might shiver
"Watch out you kids or I'll bust your liver."
And thirdly, would quote with a monstrous sigh
"Every dern one of ye's skin your eyes."

Many botanists and field naturalists, seeking information, came to see our Dad. Big brother and sister were permitted to guide the visitors to a special floating bog where the pitcher plants and some of the more rare orchids grew. A search for an uncommon fragrant fern at Rainbow Lake had a humorous twist. The visiting botanists were gazing high up at a clump growing on a steep cliff debating how they could get up to take a photograph when someone said, "What is at your feet?" It was more of the same fern!

Big brother was the birdwatcher of the family. His 1915 bird list included a yellow-headed blackbird and a nest of a black-backed three-toed woodpecker.

The family was anxious to do something toward the World War I effort. Since the hospitals needed more absorbent bandaging material the medical corps had suggested sterilized sphagnum moss. With great zeal we made trip after trip to nearby bogs and filled several large bags with fresh sphagnum. The moss was spread out in a sunny spot behind the shelter hut to dry. It was astonishing to discover that it took such a quantity of damp moss to fill one bag with the dry. With a great feeling of accomplishment the family took them over to the station and watched the station master tag the bags and put them on the train.

The Robinson family always felt a little sad as the end of

August began getting closer and we would have to leave. Our greatest ambition was to be able some day to stay long enough to see the fall colours and the ultimate goal would have been a winter visit. But, in those days, there was no one to look after the heating of the town house. Mother and young brother, Mark Jr., spent three weeks in Algonquin one winter while the rest of the family stayed in Barrie and kept the home fires burning. However, our parents had always taught us to be practical in our thinking and we accepted the departure as inevitable.

The highlight of each summer was the visit with the Bartlett family at Cache Lake. In the earlier years the train was the accepted mode of travel but later we walked the eight miles up, had lunch, and returned on the evening train. The trek would have been much easier if the railroad engineers had thought about hikers and had placed the ties just a little wider apart. However, we interspersed the tediousness of taking short steps with trying to see who could balance and walk

Superintendent G. W. Bartlett's office. Note the carbide lamps.

one of the rails for the longest distance without falling off.

Mr. Bartlett would let us look as long and often as we wanted at his fascinating collection of animals and birds which had been mounted by the rangers. He explained the process of the gas-lighting used in both the house and office and even showed us the small building where the acetylene generator was housed.

The superintendent's house had a real bathroom. The hot water tank was heated by a special water-heater built on the front of the kitchen range. Mrs. Bartlett said such an arrangement had its drawbacks: the oven of that stove would not heat properly until the water in the tank had become really hot. Several years later when father was superintendent, we girls had to cope with this same problem during the summer. First the stove had to be stoked with good, dry hardwood to get the water tank heated, then stoked again to heat the oven. Everyone would then be warned not to take a bath until the baking was finished.

Once the family moved to Headquarters exploring by canoe was sadly curtailed. Also, our time was often taken up entertaining special guests. Cache Lake was surrounded by other interesting lakes but they could not be reached without portaging. Big brother was guiding by then and in those days no one thought girls could carry canoes, thus the pattern of summer activities changed.

There were tennis courts at the Highland Inn and since it was a favourite sport many a game was played there. But tennis, as well as the well-kept lawn and flower beds, seemed out of place at Algonquin where our previous outdoor recreation had centred around wilderness pastimes.

After recovering from a lengthy illness in 1924-25, father was advised to do outdoor work. He was posted at Cedar Lake in the northern part of the Park where the summer expeditions in this area proved to be the most adventuresome yet. The hills were higher and more rugged than in the south. The Nipissing and Petawawa rivers rushed down over the rocks with a roar—quite a contrast to the fairly tranquil rivers in the Joe Lake region. The Brent (formerly Hawkesbury) lumber company's mill was down the lake with several booms of logs anchored in front of it. An alligator puffed up and down continuously moving more log booms towards the mill. Our younger brother, who was twelve, had great fun walking on the logs and catching the eels that lurked beneath.

For the first time in all the eighteen years of family summer holidays fishing became one of the principal sports. Speckled trout were abundant in the fast-moving rivers and if one wanted a more sedentary occupation lake trout were plentiful too.

For the last two years before Dad retired in 1936, a war injury to his hip was making him almost too lame to get in and out of a canoe and his nature wanderings had to be short; therefore, it was a blessing in disguise that his advisory work kept him at a desk for a good part of each day.

Mother and Father had three years of retirement together before she suddenly slipped away. Father lived fifteen years longer, until he was 89. Each summer he spent at least a month at the Taylor Statten Camps and visited with all his Algonquin Park friends. He lived long enough to interest five of his grandchildren in outdoor activities. So successful was he that he has three professional science-oriented grandsons.

The family often think back and wonder what their future would have been like without the Algonquin summers to teach them self-reliance, to give them a zest to explore the unknown and, most of all, to have the opportunity to appreciate and be a part of the great outdoors. There have not been many families who have been so privileged.

NOTES AND SOURCES

The Time Before the Park

1 Geological Survey of Canada, Map 1256A.
2 *Geology of Algonquin Park,* by G. R. Guillet, published in 1969 by the Ontario Department of Mines.
3 "Excavations in Algonquin Park, 1971" in *Algonquin Archaeology* by Hurley, Kenyon, Lange and Mitchell, University of Toronto, Department of Anthropology Series 10, 1972.
4 *Algonquin Park Master Plan Research Data, 1968* (Provisional Plan).
5 *Report on Survey of Ottawa River,* 4th Session of the Thirteenth Parliament, 1839.
6 *Renewing Nature's Wealth.* A chapter was written by each division and Richard L. Lambert did the final compiling. Published by the Department of Lands and Forests, 1967. Information also from the J. R. Dymond museum file when the historical data was compiled in the 1940s for *Algonquin Story* by Audrey Saunders.
7 *Renewing Nature's Wealth,* pp. 167-172.

Logging in Algonquin

1 J. R. Dymond museum files, compiled in the 1940s.
2 Some lumbering terms and their meanings: cadge: a road that carries supplies; cull: a defective log that is discarded; deacon seat: a seat in front of each bunk in the sleep camp; scaler: a man who measures or scales logs and keeps a tally sheet to record the measurements; skid: to haul logs from woods to skidway; slash: debris left after cutting.
3 *Inventory of the Madawaska Improvement Company Ltd.,* R. G. Bowes, published by the Department of Lands and Forests, 1968.
4 Report on Survey of Ottawa River by William Hawkins, Deputy Provincial Surveyor, February 2, 1838.
5 *Renewing Nature's Wealth,* Chapter 3. The original source for the material was "Instructions to Governor Murray, December 12, 1763."
6 *Provisional Master Plan, Algonquin Park,* 1970.
7 *Up to Date or The Life of a Lumberman* by Capt. George S. Thompson. Metropolitan Toronto Library acquired their copy in 1920. It had been rebound and the publisher and date had been deleted. Thompson at the end of the book says, "Finished Easter Monday, April 14, 1895."
8 Description of this episode came from an unpublished manuscript, "Early Days in Dorset"; the author is A. J. Hillis. The manuscript that included this episode is in the possession of the Ontario Historical Society. Permission granted by the executive of O.H.S.
9 There are conflicting dates as to when the logs were driven down the Oxtongue to Lake of Bays and what year the logs went over the tramway. Logging was certainly taking place in 1893 and 1894; Steve Waters' diary, the 1894 session papers, Ralph Bice and George Thompson all provide the proof. However, interviews with some older Dorset residents lead us to believe

that the tramway operation took place for the first time in spring, 1895, with one log drive, but it took two springs to get all the logs over the tramway.

10 "Survey Records," Ministry of Natural Resources.
11 Unpublished Hillis manuscript.
12 Public Archives of Canada. Gilmour and Hughson papers (M.G. 28, III, 6, Vol. 121), File 6.
13 Unpublished Hillis manuscript.

From Tote Road to Highway

1 From *Camping in the Muskoka Region* by James Dickson, published by the Ontario Department of Lands and Forests, 1959.
2 Mark Robinson's diary.
3 Personal communication with Rose Thomas.
4 Personal communication with L.W. Hawkes, who worked on the construction of Highway 60.
5 Personal communication with Dr. Fred Fry and Nigel Martin. The Avery family has always worked in either logging or supplying tourists' needs. They are well-known for their snowshoes and paddles.
6 *A Cool Curving World* by Richard Miller, published by Longmans Canada, 1962.
7 Personal communication with Dr. Donald MacRae, Director of David Dunlap Observatory, University of Toronto.

Forest Rangers and Other Staff

1 From *Algonkin: Forest and Park,* a letter from Kirkwood to T. B. Pardee, Commissioner of Crown Lands for Ontario, August 1886.
2 Letter to A. S. Hardy from James Dickson.
3 "Some Recollections of Tom Thomson and Canoe Lake" by R. P. Little. Little spent several months in the park from 1913 to 1920 recuperating from an illness. Printed in *Culture* XVL, (1955, pp. 200-208).
4 The Honourable Frank Cochrane announced on February 10, 1910, in the *Globe* that the management of the Park would be given authority to kill beaver: "One thousand could be killed and they would never be missed."
5 Steve Waters' 1911 diary.
6 This is one of nine stories told by Mark Robinson in the 1940s, recorded by Ronald H. Perry, Headmaster of Rosseau Lake School and author of *The Canoe and You.* The stories have not previously appeared in print.
7 Another of the stories recorded by R. Perry.

Protecting the Forest

1 *Geographical Distribution of Forest Trees in Canada* by Robert Bell, Toronto, 1897, p. 297.
2 *Renewing Nature's Wealth,* Chapter 11.
3 Personal communication with F. A. MacDougall.

Wilderness Lodges and Camps

1 In 1896 A. W. Fleck, son-in-law of J. R. Booth, and treasurer of the Canada Atlantic Railway, bought 5,000 acres at sixty cents an acre from the St. Anthony Lumber Company. The land bordered on Rock Lake and included the islands off-shore. More than half this property was sold back to the St. Anthony Lumber Company in 1903 but a sizeable estate still remained. A summer home, "Men-Wah-Tay," was erected in 1898. When the daughter, Mrs. George Barclay, took over the estate, it was locally known as the Barclay Estate.
2 Personal communication with Ranger Tom Murdoch.
3 Personal communication with Mrs. Daphne Crombie. The Crombies were at Mowat for four months in 1917.
4 Mark Robinson's diary.
5 Personal communication with Nina Millen.
6 Personal communication with J. A. (Sandy) Coutts.

Canoeing and Camping

1 James Wilson's report, 1894, to A. S. Hardy, Commissioner of Crown Lands.
2 Steve Waters' diary of 1897. Also personal communication with Dr. George Marcy.
3 American tourists made these statements more than once when talking to Mark Robinson.
4 James Wilson's expense account on return from the Algonquin survey trip—in the J. R. Dymond files at the museum.
5 Personal communication with Ralph Bice.
6 George Rowe told this story many times and Mark Robinson used the incident to emphasize how important it was to trust one's guide and his decisions.
7 Personal communication with girl who had been lost. She said she hadn't been frightened. She drank a great amount of water and hadn't been hungry.
8 Personal communication.
9 Mark Robinson's own experience.

Forests, Fish and Wildlife

1 Personal communication with Professor Dwight, who even though over ninety clearly remembered each detail.
2 Personal communication.
3 Personal communication with the late George Holmberg, Dr. Fred Fry and Nigel Martin.
4 R.G. 1, Series V (Land files, 1853-1915) Surveys, Archives of Ontario.
5 Mark Robinson had an itemized list of the years parent bass were planted in certain lakes. Lake of Two Rivers was not mentioned but it would be easy for the bass in Cache Lake to migrate down the Madawaska to Lake of Two Rivers.
6 D. Simkin, Big Mammal Wildlife biologist with Ministry of Natural Resources.
7 Superintendent Bartlett's 1917 annual report.
8 *The Raven*, Vol. 5, (2), 1964.

9 Samuel de Champlain's travels (Biggar, 1922, 1925) Volume II, p. 127, June 25, 1610.
10 Present day biologists who have studied the otter intensively believe that, even though this animal has very strong neck muscles, it would hardly be likely that the ice was that thick out where the otter was observed. Possibly it was three-quarters of an inch thick near the shore where Waters was standing.
11 Taken from letters written by the late Dr. R. P. Little, Columbus, Ohio, to his sister, Alene Little.
12 Personal communication.
13 Personal communication with Colin Farmer.
14 *The Raven*, Vol. 12, No. 9 (1971).

Algonquin Artists

1 John Taylor, Ontario College of Art. Ranger O'Leary's own "saying" as known and repeated by some of the earlier rangers.
2 Personal communication with the Thomson family. All other data was collected when the book *Tom Thomson: The Algonquin Years* was written in 1969 by Ottelyn Addison in collaboration with Elizabeth Harwood.
3 Personal communication with Mrs. William Hughes.
4 *Taylor Statten* by C. A. Edwards, 1960. By permission of Adele Statten Ebbs.

PHOTOGRAPH CREDITS

Dr. E. A. Addison: 99 (right), 100, 113 (bottom), 114 (top), 115 (right), 119.
Ottelyn Addison: 46 (top right), 128 (top).
W. D. Addison: 12, 70, 86, 87, 106 (margin), 115 (left), 117 (lower), 139.
Art Gallery of Ontario: 123, 124.
Robert Bateman: 129 (bottom).
Frank Braucht: 129 (top).
Mrs. F. Calvert: 22, 24 (bottom), 37 (left).
Canadian Magazine and Ministry of Natural Resources: 41.
Canadian National Railways' Archives: 76 (top).
Mrs. Pat Cannon: 74 (bottom), 77.
Mrs. Geraldine Churchill (from Mr. R. R. Sallows' collection): 21 (bottom), 26, 27, 74 (top left), 90 (margin), 108 (margin).
Mary Colson Clare: 72 (margin), 107.
Mrs. Daphne Crombie: 79.
Aubrey Dunne: 81 (top).
Dr. Harry and Mrs. Adele Ebbs: 83, 84, 85.
A. Edmison: 81 (margin), 117 (top).
H. S. Fullerton: 36.
Ario Gatti: 99 (left).
G. B. Hayes: 14.
George Hayhurst: 65.
Mrs. William Hughes: 10 (top), 40, 127 (bottom and margin).
Stan Losee: 122.

Thoreau MacDonald: 128 (top).
Dr. George Marcy: 28, 30 (bottom), 42, 88, 90 (top).
Ministry of Natural Resources: 3, 6, 10 (margin), 16, 17 (top and bottom), 19 (top), 25, 34, 37 (right), 53 (top), 62, 66, 69, 72 (top), 94 (top), 97 (bottom), 98, 105, 110 (margin), 114 (lower), 120, 126 (top).
Mrs. Zeph Nadon: 93.
Ontario College of Art: 121, 122 (margin).
Mary McCormick Pigeon: 13, 24 (top), 35 (margin), 64 (top).
Charlie Plewman: 80.
Mrs. Ann Prewitt: 98 (top).
Public Archives of Canada: 127 (top).
Mark Robinson file: 20, 21 (top), 35 (top), 39, 44, 45, 46 (top left and margin), 48, 50, 52, 54, 56, 57, 59, 64 (bottom), 70, 73, 75, 77 (bottom), 78, 91, 95 (bottom), 97 (top), 106 (top), 109, 111, 123 (top), 117 (margin), 126 (margin), 131, 132, 134, 135, 137.
Professor H. U. Ross: 31, 32 (top and bottom), 33, 63.
R. R. Sallows: 74 (top right), 113 (top).
Donald Smith: 53 (margin).
Mrs. Patricia Swann: 30 (top), 43, 55, 94 (margin), 96, 108 (bottom), 110 (top).
Thomson Family: 23.
University of Toronto, David Dunlap Observatory: 38.
University of Toronto, Faculty of Forestry: 19 (bottom), 102.